I Want to be the Best Mom in the World....

So Then Why Do I Feel Like the Worst?

Connie Gilbride

Great Plains Ministry, Inc.
Sioux Falls, SD

Cover cartoon© by Ron Wheeler. His pen said in picture what my pen said in words. Thanks, Ron, for your generous spirit and God-given talent.

Cover design by Emily Raymond of Dakota Printing, Sioux Falls, SD. Thank you, Jesus, for giving Emily the vision to put it all together. Thank you, Emily, for blessing us.

To receive additional copies contact:
Great Plains Ministry
5907 Wren Place
Sioux Falls, SD 57107-1446
(605) 334-3384

I Want to be the Best Mom in the World...
So Then Why Do I Feel Like the Worst?

By Connie Gilbride

ISBN 0-9657485-0-2
Printed in the United States of America
by Hanes and Thomas Printers, Las Vegas, NV

CONTENTS

i

Dedication

My life is dedicated to my Lord and Savior, Jesus Christ. Thank you for dying so that I might live.

My lifelong love and commitment is dedicated to my husband, Mike. I love you. Thank you for being my greatest supporter.

My deep gratitude and thanks is dedicated to the best Mom in the whole world for me -- Delores Vilhauer. Mom, you have always been an example to me of unselfish love.

My highest respect is dedicated to my mother-in-law, Beth Gilbride. Mom, although Heaven is now your home, your life and your witness continue to bless me.

My unconditional love is dedicated to Matthew, the best son in the whole world. The name Matthew means 'a gift from the Lord'. Matt, that is truly what you are to me. I pray that Jesus continues to teach me every day how to be the best Mom in the world for you.

This book is dedicated to all Moms who have experienced the joys, fears and tears of motherhood. To you I say, "Remember, you are never alone."

Special Thanks

To Lew and Sandy Shaffer -- Ted and Barbara Platt (Co-Directors of Son Shine Ministries): Thank you for teaching me to put Jesus first. You changed my life with that simple truth.

To those whose generous and loving gifts made this book possible: I offer praise and thanksgiving to Jesus for the miraculous way He provided through you. Thank you for believing this message was important enough to share.

To Rick and Becky Youngmark: Your major financial contribution was a giant step in faith. Your obedience to Jesus blessed me and many others who will read this book. Together, we say: "All glory goes to God!"

A letter from Mike:

I have prayed that all of Jesus' greatest blessings will be poured out upon you as you read this book. I want you to know that this is an anointed work of God. I can make this statement - knowing it to be true -- because Jesus said it was. I was blessed by this book. Initially, my sole purpose in reading it was as a 'final proof' before we sent it to the printer. When finished, I came away with a deeper love and respect for my wife, Connie.

In writing this book, her desire has been to be obedient to Christ. This she has done and in this, she has brought glory to God the Father. I believe, with all of my heart, that He is pleased with this book.

I also know there will be times when you will stop reading this book. You may be hurt, offended or not believe what Connie is saying. I ask you to press on -- to allow Jesus to minister to you and bless you -- as He did with me. I have also prayed that if you put this down, you will someday pick it back up and finish reading it.

This book is an instrument of ministry. Allow Jesus to use it in your life to minister to you as a mother.

In Christ,
Mike

To my wife, Connie: Jesus has shown and taught you so much as you submitted to His lordship in your life. I'm so thankful that He chose you as my 'helpmate'.

I love you,
Mike

Introduction

I Want to be the Best Mom in the World -

So Then Why Do I Feel Like the Worst ??....

Every woman, including me, dreams of being the best Mom in the world. After all, I'm from the June Cleaver -- *Leave It To Beaver* generation. Those women on TV were the perfect Moms. They had homemade cookies waiting after school. They always had the right words to say in a crisis. Their children came to them for advice. TV and magazines bombarded me every day with role models of the perfect Mom. I wanted to be the best Mom in the whole world, too. I'm not exactly sure I can tell you when I first felt like the worst.

It could have been shortly after I found out I was pregnant. You know how it goes. Once you get over the initial elation of being pregnant -- reality hits. This 'baby-thing' was not just a dream or a wish. It was real life and I was going to be a real Mom. I wanted to be the best -- but what if I couldn't do it? What if I turned out to be the worst?

Oh, have no doubts. I loved him from the minute I saw him. He was so beautiful and every finger and toe was perfect. He was more than I ever thought or dreamed he would be. I knew I had to be the best Mom in the world for this precious gift. His arrival seemed to wash away all my doubts about being a good Mom until...we brought our precious baby home from the hospital. All of a sudden there wasn't anyone there to tell me what to do, what might work and what obviously wouldn't. As a Mom, I was now on my own and every mistake seemed to have my name on it.

I could have started feeling like the worst Mom in the world after our son, Matt, spent nights of endless crying caused by chronic ear infections. I couldn't make things

1

better. I couldn't make the pain go away. Isn't that what Moms are supposed to do -- make things better? Yes, that's when it first began.

No, maybe that feeling didn't arrive on the scene until he was in grade school and we sat down to the usual nightly ritual of homework. Surely that must have been the first time I felt like the worst Mom in the world. We had endured what seemed like hours of battle. I wanted round letters and correct spelling. He wanted a quick exit and time with his friends. Children were supposed to adore their mothers and seek their wisdom. I was sure I had read that somewhere. Why couldn't I do it? I must be the worst Mom!

No, no -- this time I have it! I started feeling like the worst Mom in the whole world the day our son's hormones kicked in. It was the day dreaded 'puberty' entered our home. I embarrassed him. I said all the wrong things around his friends. I could do nothing right. That's the day I first felt as if I was a failure. I'm sure of it!

On second thought, maybe it all began the day our son confidently left home after high school graduation. As he broke free of our tender clutches, my stomach churned. I remembered just a few short days ago when I still had to remind him to pick up his socks and brush his teeth. Our son wasn't prepared to face that big, cruel world out there. I hadn't done my job to prepare him for all he needed to know! I must be the worst Mom in the whole world.

Truthfully, I can't tell you the day I first started feeling like the worst Mom in the world. I just know somewhere along the line -- the thought began to nag at me. Maybe you've felt it, too. I have great news for you, Mom! You're not alone. We're all in this together. Most of us struggle with the same insecurities and doubts. We've all made mistakes. We've all blown it a time or two.

So as you read this book, remember I am not writing this as an authority on motherhood. My hope is through this book, you will be able to pull back the curtains and take a look inside our home. My mistakes will be obvious -- my struggles real. Most of all, I want you to see how Jesus was my constant companion. I want you to concentrate more on the great victories in my life through Jesus Christ. I pray this book will be an encouragement to you as you try to be the best Mom in the world for your children. Remember, Jesus will be there for you, too.

1

I Want to be the Best Mom in the World - So Then Why Do I Feel Like the Worst ??...

Because I Feel Like It!

Now isn't that true -- because we <u>feel</u> like it. Normally when we are feeling like the worst Mom in the whole world, it's not because someone took a huge door to door survey and we came up with the highest number of votes. It's usually difficult to explain to anyone exactly why we feel that way. Personally, I can't pinpoint the cause, but I do know some days I just...just...just <u>feel</u> like it! It's just a feeling!

That's it! It's just a feeling. So, if it's just a feeling, why does it bother me so much? Why can't I just brush it off?

What Are Feelings?

What exactly are feelings and what makes them so powerful? We can define feelings as emotions, such as love, hate, fear or anger. Most women will agree they are a powerful force, with the ability to render a totally capable Mom into a quivering mass of fear and indecision. They are even known to transform a calm, controlled Mom into an irrational, screaming machine.

Why Were We Made This Way?

I'm not sure if you've noticed but most men don't seem to battle their feelings in the same way we do. They appear to be able to separate themselves from their feelings. Women, on the other hand, find feelings are integrated into their whole lives. Those emotions seem to rule so much of everything they do and say -- or at least have a great effect.

3

Well, ladies -- God knew what He was doing when He made us emotionally sensitive. He created in us a tenderness and an ability to love. He placed in us a desire to be intimately connected to those we hold close. You see -- God didn't make any mistakes when He created us. He made us with the capability to feel deeply.

It is when our carnal, human nature gets a hold of our feelings that they are out of the control of the Holy Spirit. This is the point in which feelings are no longer being used as God intended.

In the Beginning

Let's take a look back at the very beginning when everything was created. In Colossians 1:15-16 (TLB), we see Paul is talking about Jesus. He says, "Christ is the exact likeness of the unseen God. He existed before God made anything at all, and, in fact, Christ himself is the Creator who made everything in heaven and earth..." This verse tells me Jesus was there at creation. He is, in fact, the Creator.

It goes on to say, "...all (things) were made by Christ for His own use and glory." The phrase, "made by Christ", tells me all things were created by Him. "For His own use" means He has a purpose for everything in Creation. He has a plan for everything. The phrase, "for His glory" means everything in Creation will bring Him honor and praise. Even emotions? Yes, even our emotions can bring Him glory.

How can this be? How can He use such wild, unpredictable things as emotions and feelings for His glory? How can He say they will bring Him glory?

Jesus can say it because He, too, experienced emotions when He became a man and came to earth to live. He also made Himself vulnerable to every earthly feeling, temptation and experience. He understood emotions, not just because He created them but because He experienced them and knew them firsthand. Jesus felt anger at the temple moneychangers (Matthew 21:12). He wept at the death of his friend, Lazarus (John 11:35).

Jesus experienced emotions, just as we do; yet, He was not ruled by them. I believe He wants the same for us. He doesn't want us to be ruled by them either. This means we need to let Him rule our emotions and feelings.

4

God's Way vs. the World's Way

First we need to understand there are always two ways of looking at everything -- the world's way and God's way [1]. The same is true of emotions. For example, let's take a look at anger. The world's way of looking at anger is the hateful, vindictive feeling that destroys. God's way of looking at anger is the righteous anger over sin. God loves us and because He loves us, He also hates sin. (Romans 12:9, "Love must be sincere. Hate what is evil; cling to what is good.") We also see that we are to follow His example. John 13:34 says, "...Love one another. As I have loved you, so you must love one another." We need to love others in the same way that God loves us. And this is how God loves us: "But God demonstrates His own love for us in this: while we were still sinners, Christ died for us" (Romans 5:8). Simply, it is hating the sin but loving the sinner. God hated the sin in us but while we were still sinners, He loved us enough to send His Son to die for us so that our sin could be erased. When anger is handled in this way, it does not destroy the individual but it also does not condone sinful behavior.

Now, to be truthful, I sometimes have a difficult time separating the two. I seem to get the sin and the sinner intertwined in my feelings, letting the anger center in on the person. I especially had a hard time with our son, Matt, in this area. He would do something wrong and KABLOOEY -- he was the target of my anger. I was dealing with anger the world's way -- it destroyed and tore down Matt instead of just hating the sin he had committed.

If you are a Mom who is prone to outbursts of anger, this may be the feeling or emotion that rules your life. You have probably tried to stop screaming at your kids. You may have vowed to change your ways -- to quit losing your temper but it keeps happening again and again. It's because in our own strength, we will never be able to control our emotions. It's much like trying in our own power to control our tongue.

I believe what the Bible says when it tells us about prayer. Philippians 4:6 says, "Do not be anxious about anything, but in everything, by prayer and petition, with thanksgiving, present your requests to God." I believe The Living Bible

---

[1] Ministers' Handbook, Lewis F. Shaffer, Son Shine Ministries Int'l, 1991, p81

says it very simply: "Don't worry about anything; instead pray about everything..." (TLB). The Bible also says that as His child, I can hear His voice. (John 10:27, "My sheep listen to My voice; I know them and they follow me.") This reminds me I can pray and <u>ask</u> Him why I am feeling angry and He <u>will answer</u>. Many times our own anger is just a signal of something deeper that Jesus wants to reveal.

I can also ask Him how He wants me to deal with the anger. He holds all the wisdom and knowledge and the Bible tells me it is mine for the asking (Colossians 2:2-3). I also know He said He would send His Holy Spirit to empower and enable me to do what He tells me to do. "Now to Him who is able to do immeasurably more than all we ask or imagine, according to His power that is at work within us" (Ephesians 3:20). He says He will even do more than I expect.

I don't need to be the way I've always been. I don't need to let anger rule me, nor do you. He says that His power is at work within us to change us.

Fear Ruled My Life

In my case, not anger but the emotion of fear was the overriding force that ruled my life. As a young child I was afraid of falling and getting hurt. As a teen, it was my fear of being rejected that kept me away from people. I never took risks. I always played it safe because fear kept me captive. When our son arrived on the scene, the fear he would be hurt or even die was constantly on my mind. If you've ever battled with feelings of fear, you understand what a powerful force it can be.

Everyday, I would pledge -- "Today I am not going to be afraid!" I put on my tough, defensive face as I watched Matt go out the front door of the house to walk to school. I could visibly see him cross an open field and enter the school playground. With my eyes, I could see that he was safe but the further he walked from our front door, the more fear began to creep into my mind. This feeling of fear ballooned until I "knew" he was dead -- even though I saw him still walking. Even logic could not talk me out of my fear.

Fear seemed to always start as a small ripple of doubt, much like a wave, beginning to lick at my toes. Soon, it was splashing up to my waist and then swelled to a monumental wave engulfing my entire body. Fear ruled my life. That was the world's way of looking at fear -- it frightened all who

6

would listen to its call. Fear frightened me almost to the point of incapacitation. It paralyzed me!

It's an Attention-Getter

God's way of looking at fear is often much different from ours. 2 Timothy 1:7 says God does not give us a spirit of fear. That's true. Yet, I believe He allows us to experience or feel fear many times to warn us or give us discernment in a particular situation. It's an attention-getter.

A few years ago, my husband, Mike and I were in Europe for several weeks, ministering at military bases. Matt was back in Texas attending high school. Now, he had a dependable family supervising him, so there should be nothing to cause me to fear. Right?

One night, I woke up with a strange sense of danger. It just nagged at me enough so I couldn't get back to sleep. The more I thought about it -- the more that little ripple of fear began to grow. Soon it was a great, huge wave of fear that engulfed me. I knew something was wrong with Matt. My imagination went wild. Was he in a car accident? Was he lying dead somewhere? It was three in the morning in Germany -- which meant it was early evening in America. I felt as if I needed to get up right then and call Matt to check on him. I couldn't stand it any longer. I woke up Mike and explained my fear and asked if we should call home.

Now, I have to tell you, my husband really wants to do what God wants him to do. It means there may be times when he must tell me 'no' in order to tell God 'yes'. He earnestly prayed about what we should do. He said he knew we were not to call right then but he reached over and held me as he prayed for Matt and for me. He hugged me and said it would be all right, then promptly rolled over and went back to sleep. "Wait a minute!" "Wait a minute!" I'm not done worrying!" "I don't 'feel' any better!" How could he just fall back asleep when our son was probably dying or even worse! The fear continued to plague me.

I struggled and struggled with that fear until I finally remembered something wonderful that a great teacher and man of God taught me. Lew Shaffer always said, "Your feelings are like a barometer -- they should get your attention to tell you something is happening." That's true! I didn't even have to decide what that something was. I could ask Jesus (remember 'pray about everything'). After all, Jesus

7

didn't create feelings to drive us crazy with worry. The Bible says that He plans to use them for His use and His glory.

So, I told Jesus I was fearful (as if He didn't already know). I then asked Him why I was feeling that way. (I believe He used the feeling of fear to get my attention so I would come to Him and ask Him what was happening.) He said it was to remind me to pray for Matt. He told me to pray Matt would find comfort during this time. Now, that didn't exactly make me 'feel' less fearful. It made me wonder <u>why</u> our son would need comfort in the first place!

At the same time, it reminded me of Jesus in the Garden of Gesthemene, when He prayed so fervently He sweat great drops of blood. He said to the Father, "...if it is possible, may this cup be taken from me. Yet not as I will, but as you will" (Matthew 26:39). Since He was sweating great drops of blood, it tends to make me believe that Jesus didn't exactly 'feel' peaceful in the garden -- but He was obedient. I didn't exactly 'feel' peaceful that night in Germany but I knew I had to be obedient to do what Jesus told me to do. I prayed that Matt would be comforted. I soon drifted off to sleep.

I eagerly approached the next morning. I was ready to call Matt to make sure everything was all right. When I asked Mike, he said he had been praying about calling Matt but Jesus told him, "Not today." (My heart screamed, "You're kidding! -- Not today?") The fear started to creep in again. Jesus reminded me to pray for Matt to be comforted, as He told me to pray the night before.

This scenario went on for two days until finally Mike said, "Call Matt." I couldn't fly to the phone fast enough. When he answered, I said, "How are you doing, Son?" "Better today, Mom." "Honey, what was the matter?" "Well, Mom, my girlfriend broke up with me but I'm doing better now. Jesus brought me through it." "Matt, when did that happen?", I asked. "Two nights ago, Mom." Two nights ago -- exactly the time when I woke up in the middle of the night, full of fear.

Who Will Be Their Rescue?

Now, Mothers, some of you are probably saying, "No way! If that happened to me, I don't care what my husband said. I would have called my child!" I want you to see if I would have called Matt when my emotions and feelings were telling me to, <u>I</u> would have been his rescue. <u>I</u> would have

8

made him feel better. There are times when Jesus uses Mothers to do just that -- make our children feel better. I also want you to see just how unreliable our feelings are and how reliable Jesus is. By waiting to call until Jesus said the time was right, He became Matt's rescue -- not me. Remember Matt said, "Jesus brought me through it." I was praying as Jesus told me to pray -- that Matt would be comforted. Jesus did comfort him through a very difficult time. Matt drew closer to Jesus and so did I. Mom, it is important to remember as our children grow into young adults, they need to grow away from dependence on us and learn to depend on Jesus. He is always with them -- even when we can't be.

Is fear a constant presence in your life? Romans 8:15 says, "For you did not receive a spirit that makes you a slave again to fear, but you received the Spirit of sonship. And by Him we cry, 'Abba, Father'." As a child of His, We can cry out to our Father. We don't have to let feelings of fear rule our lives. Jesus can teach us a new way -- His way to deal with fear.

Do You Battle with Guilt?

Let's look at another powerful emotion -- guilt. Do you battle with feelings of guilt? Join the club -- most of us do. I especially struggled with guilty feelings when our son left home after high school graduation. That's when I realized I couldn't fix all the things I had done wrong when he was growing up. I began to look back at being his Mom with deep regrets.

Before Matt was born, I would dream of his perfect little room. Everything would be coordinated and arranged just like in the magazines. When he finally arrived, he didn't get that teddy bear border all around his room. He slept in a used crib, wore lots of hand-me-downs and even had to have our guest bed in the room with him. (Guilt says, "If you had really wanted to, you could have found a way to make his room perfect, Connie. You're so selfish! You just didn't care enough like other Moms.")

I was working full time and I was so tired by evening that I often fell asleep as I sat beside him at night to read him his bedtime story. (Guilt says, "What kind of Mom is too tired to read to her own precious little child? She must be the worst Mom around!")

9

During the grade school years, I snapped and nagged at him for not cleaning up his room. (Guilt says, "Don't you know there was a way to correct him without destroying him? What kind of Mom are you?")

Those teen years were difficult for me. Matt didn't want me at school helping with the graduation party or bake sales. (Guilt says, "Other kids don't mind their mothers being around. You must be a terrible Mom or he'd want you there!")

Guilt. It's usually the result of a hurt we are feeling. I was hurt and wounded when I looked back at the job I'd done as a Mom. That hurt made me feel guilty. (You could call it a form of self-pity.) "I'm so terrible. I didn't do a good job of being a mother." This is definitely the world's way of turning hurt into guilt.

What guilt does is get our eyes focused down on ourselves. When I look down, all I see is myself -- no one else -- not even Jesus. This tunnel vision creates a sense of hopelessness and can even lead to depression. I know this is not Jesus' will for me. I know this is not His purpose or use for my feelings.

Don't Take It

Thirty-four times in the Bible, Satan is called the accuser.[2] Revelation 12:10 says he accuses us before our God day and night. I can just picture him at the throne of God throwing around accusations about me. "God - don't you see what a terrible Mom she is? Look at all her mistakes. Why - she even admits them herself. What a weak person you placed down there!"

At the same time he's accusing at the throne, I hear those accusations in my ear. The accuser is constantly poking and prodding me, trying to offer his accusations as if they were some tempting chocolate - a gift from him - rather than the lies they really are. "Here, Connie. Take these. You know they are true and everybody else can see that they're true. You might as well accept them!"

Recently, I've started to understand they are only accusations, charges or complaints against me. They are

---

[2] Vines Expository Dictionary of Biblical Words, W.E. Vine, Ed., Thomas Nelson Publishers, 1985, p10-11

much like a gift. It doesn't belong to me until I reach out my hand and accept them. Once I accept them, they become mine -- something I own. At the point of acceptance, it changes from an accusation to guilt. Let's go back and read all of Revelation 12:10. "Then I heard a loud voice in heaven say: 'Now have come the salvation and the power and the kingdom of our God, and the authority of His Christ. For the accuser of our brothers, who accuses them before our God day and night, has been hurled down'." When the end comes, Satan will be hurled down -- defeated. His accusations will be rendered powerless -- worth absolutely nothing because he can no longer destroy me. He will be destroyed. The next time the accuser tries to offer you his gift of guilt -- remember the end of the story. He loses!

Ephesians 6:11 gives us Godly wisdom in our battle against guilt: "Put on the full armor of God so that you can take your stand against the devil's schemes." Don't fall for his accusations. When he offers guilt -- stand firm and pull back your empty hand. Don't take it!

Hurt Feelings Have Been Around for Awhile

The opportunity for feeling hurt was not foreign to Jesus. Don't you think He was probably feeling hurt over the way the people treated Him? Even those who welcomed Him on Palm Sunday, turned their backs on Him when Good Friday arrived. In the midst of people spitting on Him and whipping Him -- don't you think He probably felt hurt over their reaction? All He was trying to do was to help them? Jesus was God who came down to earth as man to rescue His people.

He could have responded as the world says we should respond to hurt. He could have felt self-pity and guilt. He could have said, "What did I do wrong? Why didn't I just say it another way -- then maybe they would have listened to me? Oh, poor me!"

That was not His Father's way of using hurt and Jesus understood that. The hurt Jesus was feeling was because He felt the sins of the world on His shoulders. He felt the hurt of unrepentant sin as He was beaten. He was not distracted by His feelings of hurt but centered on the real problem -- the sins of the people.

11

Move Past the Hurt

When we are rejected, criticized or wounded by others, we can let Jesus use the hurt in the same way. At these times, we don't have to just react. We have the perfect opportunity to ask Jesus how He wants us to feel about what has happened.

If we are feeling hurt over the way somebody treated us, this is our chance to turn to Jesus. He will give us the strength and love to forgive and not turn the hurt into self-pity.

Yes, I didn't do a perfect job of being a Mom. You probably didn't either. So, if there is an area of sin -- something we did or didn't do -- this is a great opportunity to come to Him to seek forgiveness and find freedom from the guilt. He offers forgiveness freely and generously.

Isn't this great news? We don't have to wallow in guilt. We can move past the hurt.

Acting Out of Guilt

Sometimes we do things _for_ our children that make _us_ feel good. I used to think making chocolate chip cookies from scratch rather than buying cookies was a must, even when Matt would rather have had my undivided attention and a package of Oreos ™. My reasoning was all the best Moms baked cookies from scratch -- so therefore, I had to. I did it out of guilt. We could be buying our children everything they want because we just aren't spending the time with them that we know we should. It is a way we sometimes try to buy away the guilt. Some of us won't tell our children 'no' because we don't want them to get mad at us. After all, if they got mad at us, we would certainly feel like the worst Mom in the whole world.

Moms, sometimes we do things for our children that keep _us_ from feeling guilty! Some of those things may not be the best thing for our child and may not be God's will for them. We may even use them to buy our way out of feeling guilty.

Remember Jesus knows better than anyone what our children need. We can ask Him what to give them and do for them. Jesus doesn't work on the 'guilt principle'. He works on the 'love principle'. He loves our children so much that

He never gives out of guilt. He will enable you to give in the same way. Just ask Him.

God Has a Purpose for Guilt

Yes, God does have a purpose for guilt. John 16:8 says, "When He (the Holy Spirit) comes, He will convict the world of guilt in regard to sin and righteousness and judgment." The Holy Spirit's purpose for guilt is to convict us of the sin in our lives and to show us how to become (righteous) right with God even though we deserve eternal punishment as our judgment. God's uses guilt to move in our hearts and cause us to come to repentance. When we repent, we are forgiven and set free from guilt. Guilt is no longer the prison that Satan intends it to be -- locking us in and holding us captive. It is instead, the door to freedom that Jesus offers.

Satan's plan for guilt is to destroy. Satan is plotting and planning your destruction by trying to get you to hang on to that guilt. If you've confessed your sin to God -- He has forgiven you and His purpose for the guilt is complete. It's over. So, if you're still feeling guilty after you've confessed your mistakes - that guilt is not from God. God's perfect plan is to use guilt to rebuild and renew us in His forgiving grace and love.

I've Got That Joy, Joy, Joy, Joy...

Oh, I've had that joy, joy, joy! Now, isn't joy a great emotion to have around! I was excited and bubbling with happiness when Matt came home from school with great grades. I was exuberant when he cleaned his room without being told ninety times! (I was so happy that I must have finally done something right. I must be a good Mom to get my child to behave like that!)

However, I wasn't too thrilled when he sassed back. I felt far from happy when he told a lie. I felt as if my happiness was on a roller coaster ride. I was up when things were going great and way down when things were going wrong. That's not joy -- that's happiness. Happiness can be found in circumstances and events. It can cause you to take a wild ride on the crest of emotions and feelings. I guess you could call it a 'joyride'.

This is not God's way of looking at joy. Joy isn't a result of how we feel. Joy is because of who Jesus is. If you have

13

personally recognized your helplessness as a sinner and believe through His death He provided your rescue; He is your Savior. He is my Savior, too. He saved us from hell. This fact alone should bring us pure joy that never ends. He is our Shepherd -- He guides us wherever we go. He has promised we will never be alone and this should bring us joy unceasing. He is our Provider. He gives us all we need. This should bring us an everlasting joy. It is because of who He is that we are joyful.

Who's Responsible for My Joy?

It is not our child's responsibility to make us joyful (You're kidding!). It's not even our husband's job. (Are you surprised?) We can't even blame our circumstances for causing us to lose our joy. (Darn!) Ladies, isn't is about time that we quit acting as if they do? Nothing has to affect our joy because Jesus is our joy. This is how we can dare look at everything that happens in our life as a joy. Just as James 1:2 says, "Consider it pure joy, ... whenever you face trials of many kinds, because you know that the testing of your faith develops perseverance."

Joy is Not a Reaction to How I Feel

Does it mean we're never sad? No. Of course, there can be sadness. It may be a necessary feeling to bring us through a time of grief or pain. Sadness can be a normal and necessary reaction. The important thing to remember is at the end of the sadness is an unswerving joy that rests in Jesus. Does it mean we are never discouraged by the behavior of our children? No, but it does mean we don't have to lose hope. This is exactly what prolonged discouragement can bring -- a sense of hopelessness. When our joy rests in Jesus, we never have to feel hopeless.

Do we always feel joyful? No, but joy is not a feeling -- it is a choice. Do you know many times I have to choose to be joyful? I'm not talking about putting on a plastic face and smiling my way through the day in self denial. No, I'm talking about choosing to turn to Jesus in the midst of difficult times. He never changes even when my circumstances do. (Hebrews 13:8, "Jesus Christ is the same yesterday, today and forever.")

14

He never stops loving when others might. He never gives up when I have. It's my choice. I can stay and wallow in unhappiness or turn to Jesus who promises true joy. Joy doesn't always make us break out in song or smile ear to ear. Many times, joy is simply a feeling of tenderness or thankfulness in the middle of trying times. Joy is not my reaction to how I feel; it is my reaction to who Jesus is!

What Good Are They?

Dear friend, I know you want to be the best Mom in the world. When you are _feeling_ like the worst -- I offer that you ask Jesus why you are feeling that way. Then ask Him how _He_ wants you to feel. I can assure you He never says, "Today I want you to feel like the worst Mom in the whole world."

He can be trusted. Colossians 2:6 (TLB) says, "And now just as you trusted Christ to save you, trust Him too, for each day's problems; live in vital union with Him!" If you could trust Him to save you -- He can _surely_ be trusted with your feelings and emotions.

You may say, "Well, I _am_ trying to trust Him but I keep struggling with my feelings and emotions. Maybe I don't have enough faith. Maybe I'm not trusting enough."

Let's go back to Colossians 2:6. It says, "And now just as you trusted Christ to save you..." How did you come to trust Christ for your salvation? Did you grit your teeth and get determined? Did you talk yourself into it? No - the faith to trust Him for your salvation came from God. It was a gift of God given by His grace. It is in the same way we trust Him with each day's problems. It is all His doing. Rejoice in this: He is working trust in and through us - by His grace.

Emotions. Feelings. If they're so much trouble, what good are they? They are a gift from God. He plans to use them -- not to rule us -- but to turn us to His Son, Jesus.

Let's pray together:

Lord, You know how I struggle with keeping my emotions under control. I'm tired of being on this roller coaster. Help me to let go of my emotions and give them to You so you might control them. Remind me to pray and ask You how to feel and not to trust my feelings. I know through this, my faith and trust in You will increase.

In Jesus' name, I pray.
Amen.

15

*S*pend some time thinking about these questions:

1. What feelings do I struggle with the most in my life?

2. How do these emotions and feelings affect my life?

3. Describe a time when Jesus used an emotion or feeling as an attention-getter.

4. If I let Jesus have control of my emotions, how could that affect my life?

5. Am I ready to let go and put my emotions under the control of Jesus Christ?

2

I Want to be the Best Mom in the World - So Then Why Do I Feel Like the Worst ??. . .

Because I Compare Myself to Every Other Mom !

Every other Mom at church had it all together. I'd watch them happily sing songs to their children, patiently and wisely answer their 100 questions and never lose their tempers or yell at their children. To me they were examples of Godly mothers.

I Was a Mother Maniac

Then I'd look at myself -- 'Mother Maniac'. I rushed around doing a hundred other things all at the same time. I worked full time, was actively involved in church groups and social organizations and always had Matt in some type of sport or activity. We were always on the run. Some days, I'm sure he thought his middle name was 'Hurry'.

There were times he must have felt as if he was a burden to me and an interruption in my busy schedule. We sang songs together in the car on the way to the baby-sitter or as I sloshed him through the nightly bath (in between three loads of laundry and baking a cake for the church bake sale). I lost my temper and I was inconsistent in my reactions. I was always tired at the end of the day when he wasn't. It's true! It's true! I must be the worst Mom in the whole world!

I didn't see those other Moms acting like I did! They were perfect or at least almost perfect (but who's counting!).

Comparison Isn't a Godly Principle

That's just the problem! We feel like the worst Mom in the whole world because we are comparing ourselves to other Moms. We are trying to rate ourselves by holding up our performance against other Moms. Did you know that I can't find anywhere in the Bible it says, '...therefore, compare yourself against every other person to decide your worth.' I just can't find it anywhere! The Bible even speaks about the lack of wisdom of those who do compare themselves to others. In 2 Corinthians 10:12 it says, "Not that we venture to class or <u>compare</u> ourselves with some of those who commend themselves. But when they measure themselves by one another, and compare themselves by one another, they are without understanding" (RSV). This Scripture tells me that comparing ourselves to others shows we do not understand God's ways. If we are comparing ourselves to other mothers, we are without understanding -- without wisdom.

I have a dear friend, Debbie, who to me is a beautiful example of a Godly mother. She absolutely loves being pregnant and says that's when she feels the best physically. On the other hand, for me being pregnant was a wonderful experience but I can't exactly say that I 'loved' it enough to repeat it five times! She thrives on the presence of her children and never worries if the house isn't in perfect order. To her it is more important to see her children being children. She is an absolute wonder and a blessing to her five beautiful children.

Even though I knew I should relax and enjoy our little boy, I was driven by perfectionism. Although I could never seem to accomplish it -- keeping the house spotless and things in order became an obsession. Oh, how I used to look at Debbie and marvel that toys in the living room didn't bother her like they did me. She was such a relaxed Mom. I felt a little sadness because I wasn't that way -- the same as Debbie. That is, until Jesus reminded me that I'm not Debbie. I'm Connie with a Connie personality. (We're all different. That's what keeps the world interesting!)

Debbie is one of the greatest Moms I've ever met. She has some qualities that serve as a great role model for me but Jesus has shown me that I also have some great qualities. They're just not the same as any other Mom. I'm not exactly the same as Debbie. I'm me! (Remember the Scripture says don't compare yourself to others.) What a freedom that has brought to my life!

Jesus is Our Example

Although they might be a great example to me, I don't have to be just like any other Mom to be the kind of mother God wants me to be. I need to be just like Jesus. The Word of God says we are to have Jesus as our example in all we do -- even in how to be a Mom (I Peter 2:21). Now notice that we are not asked to compare ourselves to Him either but to use Him as our example -- to pattern our lives after Him. If I compared myself to Jesus, I would be in deep trouble. I would always fall short when I stand next to His perfection. This is why He stands as our example -- to show us the way.

Now, I caught you! I heard some of you mumble under your breath; "Jesus was never a mother! How could He understand! How can He show us the way to be a great Mom!" You are sharp! He never was a mother but He does understand and He can show us how to love, care for others, and forgive -- because He has done all of those things.

Jesus is the example for Moms. In addition, the qualities He demonstrates can be applied to being a mother, as well as being a good friend, wife or co-worker.

Loving His Way

How did Jesus love? Unconditionally. John 3:16 says, "For God so loved the world that He gave His one and only Son, that whoever believes in Him shall not perish but have eternal life". He didn't say, "I'll only give my Son to those who are without sin -- those who can live perfectly and do everything right." He said they only needed to believe in Him. If He loved us only if we were perfect -- we'd all be lost, wouldn't we?

I believe what He said meant this: "It doesn't matter what you've done. It doesn't matter how many mistakes you've made. I love you so much that I gave up My only Son for you. Believe in Him and you will have eternal life." That's unconditional love -- the the same kind of love He can teach us to have as a mother.

19

But, Can I Do It?

It sounds easy on paper, doesn't it? It does to me, too -- until I get home and have to put it into practice.

Matt was a sophomore in college and I was struggling with some financial decisions he made. I knew I needed to love him even if he made, what I felt was, the wrong decision. I was having a tough time separating the feelings from the facts. I knew it was a fact that I was to love him unconditionally, yet I didn't always 'feel' like loving him. My brain kept thinking, "Why isn't he more responsible with money?" "Why doesn't he plan ahead?" My heart kept saying, "Jesus wants you to love him in spite of the mistakes he makes." It became a battle between my heart and my mind.

Then, as I was driving around town doing some errands, I could hear God speak to my heart. "You're still struggling over this issue, Connie." My response was, "You're telling me!" I felt my heart begin to soften as He said, "If you want to quit struggling. You need to love Matt just the way he is." I knew it was true. I knew it in my head. I also knew I couldn't do it on my own. I had to ask Jesus to help me love Matt the way He loves Matt. You see, it just doesn't come naturally for me or for any of us to love that way but it comes through the supernatural power of Jesus Christ.

I don't want you to think this means we shouldn't expect the best from our children or not correct them when they are wrong. On the contrary. We have an obligation as parents to train our children but our love shouldn't be based on whether or not they produce a certain behavior.

Jesus will help you to love your children the way He loves -- unconditionally. Follow His example and reach out for His help.

Caring the Way He Cared

How does Jesus show us to care for others? Unselfishly -- thinking of others first. Whoa! Isn't this what we do as Mothers almost every minute of every day -- take care of everybody else first! Yes, for many of us it is, especially when our children are small and require our full attention. There were times when I resented having to take care of my husband and son, before I could take care of myself. When

Matt was small, I worked 12 hour shifts as a registered nurse. The last thing I felt like doing when I got home was thinking about someone else. I just wanted to crawl into a hot bathtub and have a Calgon ™ experience. With so many demands on my life, there were times when I coveted my own time -- to just do what I wanted to do. However, those times never seemed to happen.

Serving Requires an Attitude Check

We've all been there -- haven't we? Maybe you're there today, serving your little heart out. Let me ask you if your heart is in your service or if are you just gritting your teeth while you take care of everyone else? I believe Jesus shows us how caring for others the way He would, is more an attitude of the heart than an action. First our heart has to be right about caring and serving -- then our actions will follow. And yes, service many times will require sacrifice.
Galatians 5:13 says, "...serve one another in love." There we go, back to that unconditional love. Our attitude must be one of serving because we love. First because we love Jesus and want to follow Him. Second, because we love those He has asked us to serve.
What about those days when Matt is grouchy or disobedient? I don't have to care for him or serve him those days. Right? Wrong! It may be more of a challenge to care for him on those days but Jesus asks that I always serve in love. OK -- this means I don't have to serve anyone I don't love. Right? Wrong! It means Jesus can teach me to love even in their unlovable times. He will also teach me by His example how to serve them in love.

How Is That Possible?

How is it possible to love them when they are unlovable? How is it possible to always serve in love? We find our answer in Matthew 22:37-38: "Love the Lord your God with all your heart and with all your soul and with all your mind. This is the first and greatest commandment." This is where love must begin -- loving God first. This is why it is called the first and greatest commandment. Now it's not just a little love for God -- but a total, 'everything I've got, all-or-nothing' kind of love.

2 1

When I love God with all my heart, soul and mind -- I am able to do what verse 39 says: "...Love your neighbor as yourself." Love God first. When you love Him totally, He will give you love for others -- your neighbors. This is how we can love them in their unlovable times and serve them in love.

Does Serve Mean Be a Slave?

When Matt was about six years old, he went through a time of thinking he was the Junior King of the house. He would sit in front of the TV and yell into the kitchen -- "Mom, get me a drink!" No "please". No coming into the kitchen to get it. If I didn't move fast enough it would be followed by his best whining voice,"Mommmm - I'm thirsty!" He somehow started to think I was the slave in his little kingdom.

I am a little slow, so it took me a couple of weeks to catch on to what was happening before I called a quick halt to his royal act. I don't think Matt sat down one day and decided he would make me his slave. I believe he was just trying out a little power play, as most normal children do, and found out that it worked. He could get what he wanted by whining at his Mom. Now that's human nature -- to try to get someone else to do it for us. (Remember Tom Sawyer?) Matt just needed someone to remind him Jesus wouldn't want him to make Mom, Dad or anyone else his slave.

Mom, never let your children think you are their slave. If we care for our children and serve them in love -- we will also teach them to care for and serve others in love. We will never let them take advantage of others -- especially us. We will also teach them to follow Jesus' example.

God didn't ask us to be Mommy Martyrs. Mommy Martyrs often end up exhausted and resentful because of selfish and demanding children. These children often grow up into selfish, demanding adults because they never learned how to serve others. They only learn they are served.

Don't cheat your children. Teach them to serve others as well as to be served. It makes them better balanced adults and brings joy into their lives as they learn to serve others.

Forgive as Jesus Forgave

Jesus also shows us how to forgive. Forgiveness is an essential quality of being a mother patterned after Jesus.

It is forgiving even when we don't feel like it. Forgiving, even when the other person definitely doesn't deserve it. We have the perfect example in Jesus as He was led to the cross to be executed. He said, "Father, forgive them, for they do not know what they are doing" (Luke 23:34). Those He forgave definitely didn't deserve it but He forgave them anyway. Ephesians 4:32 says, "Be kind and compassionate to one another, forgiving each other, just as in Christ God forgave you". One of the best reasons we forgive others is because God, through Christ, forgave us.

Forgiveness is Not Just a Suggestion

In fact, we must forgive others because He forgives us. It's not just a nice suggestion we find in the Scripture but it is written as a command. Jesus gives us explicit directions in Matthew 6:14-15: "For if you forgive men when they sin against you, your heavenly Father will also forgive you. But if you do not forgive men their sins, your Father will not forgive your sins". Do you see how serious He is about forgiveness? He says, if we withhold forgiveness from others -- He will withhold forgiveness from us.

I personally believe it is so strongly stated in the Scripture because Jesus wants us to understand that the effects of unforgiveness can cripple and destroy us. Unforgiveness eats away at the heart with bitterness and begins to destroy from within. Jesus wants us to be whole. Unforgiveness is a prison -- holding us hostage to the past. Jesus wants us free. The command to forgive comes from the heart of a loving Savior.

Especially in Our Own Homes

If we follow Jesus' example, we are to exhibit that same forgiveness everywhere, especially in our own homes. Now, I understand it is not always easy to do -- but it is what Jesus commands and desires for us.

When Matt was a senior in high school, he was trying to break free from some parental control. He began to resent us as parents, saying we were too strict and were ruining his life. Matt and I were always extremely close but one day he singled me out and targeted me alone as the cause for his whole 'rotten life'. It hurt me so deeply that he would even think of saying something so mean. Eventually my hurt turned to anger. How dare he treat me like that! I'm his mother! Doesn't he know how much I've done for him? Doesn't he know how many times I gave up what I wanted so that he could have what he wanted?

Later, Matt came back to me and asked for forgiveness for the way he had acted. I didn't feel like forgiving him. I was still hurt and angry. I was still feeling the emotions he had triggered.

However, with Jesus as my example, I didn't have the option to say, "Forget it, buddy boy! I'll forgive you when I'm good and ready!" I knew I needed to be ready to forgive immediately because that is what Jesus did for me.

It was a _decision_ to forgive -- _not_ a feeling. If I had waited around until I _felt_ like forgiving Matt, it would have been awhile! The Scripture doesn't say, "Wait around until you _feel_ like forgiving..." It just says, "forgive".

So, when I said I forgave him, I opened the door for Jesus to work the forgiveness in my heart. I believe that the act of forgiving enabled Jesus to change my heart so my heart could match the words of my mouth. And that is exactly what Jesus did for me. He worked in my heart so I would let go of the hurt Matt caused and eventually 'feel' the forgiveness I had proclaimed with the words of my mouth.

Through forgiveness, Jesus restored our relationship. How freeing it was for both Matt and for me!

He Lived What He Taught

Loving. Caring. Forgiving. These are all qualities Jesus teaches us by His example. Jesus shows us how we can live, by the example of how He lived. He was not just full of words; He lived what He taught.

Jesus said, "...I have come that they may have life, and have it to the full" (John 10:10). I believe this verse means He came to give us all we need to live for Him. He fully and abundantly provides all we need to follow Him. He continues to show us the way.

Don't Go Buy a Tape Measure

Aren't you glad to hear you don't have to measure up to anyone else to be a great Mother! You don't have to compare yourself to any other Mom to see if you are qualified! Jesus only asks that you look to Him as your example. If you are feeling like the worst Mom in the whole world because you are comparing yourself to other Moms -- it is time to stop!

Take your eyes off others and all you think they are. Take your eyes off yourself and all you think you're not. It is time to place your eyes on Jesus. He doesn't demand perfection or comparison.

I can hear Him calling; "Come follow Me. I will show you the way. Don't worry about making mistakes. Don't be afraid of failing. Don't think you're not as good as other mothers. Just come follow Me."

I want you to say this out loud: "All that I'm not -- Jesus is!" Now, ask Jesus to help you believe it -- because it's true!

Our prayer:

Father, Thank You for making me. Even though I don't always feel like it, I know that You knew exactly what you were doing when you made me exactly like you did.

Take me as I am and mold me into the Mother You want me to be. I know You will do this in me as I follow the example of Your Son, Jesus, in all I do. Help me to throw away the ruler of comparison. Thank you for showing me I don't have to try to be like anyone else. I want to be more like Jesus.

                    In His name I pray.
                    Amen

In your quiet time, consider these questions:

1. Do I frequently tend to compare myself to others? If the answer is 'yes, how does that affect me?

2. What step can I take today to stop myself from using the 'comparison ruler'?

3. What one quality of Jesus mentioned in this chapter would help make me a better Mother?

3

I Want to be the Best Mom in the World - So Then Why Do I Feel Like the Worst ??....

Because I Treat Dad Like the Worst Dad in the Whole World !!

OK -- so maybe you don't treat him like the worst Dad in the whole world -- but do you treat him like the best?

Maybe you're wondering why you should treat him like the best Dad in the whole world when he doesn't always act like the best. Possibly, he's just an average Dad. Why should you treat him like the best? Isn't it the principle of 'cause and effect'? If he does a great job as a Dad, I encourage and compliment him. If he slacks off, my job is to get him back in line and tell him where he fell short, Right? Or is it?

God's Plan for Dad

Let's look at what the Bible says about Dad and how he fits into God's plan for the family. When God created Adam and Eve, He had an order to creation. He didn't just throw things together and hope that everything turned out great. He had a plan. He created man first, then woman was created out of man. This had nothing to do with who was more important or who was more talented but it had everything to do with headship. The man was not created to be the head over the woman because he was better. Man was not created as head over woman to control her or to be superior. God chose man as the head to serve as a system of protection and leadership.

He's much like the trail boss on a wagon train. His job was to lead and encourage those pioneers on toward the goal. He constantly aimed them in the right direction. He also scouted ahead and checked the trail for danger. He was the leader and protector. In the home, Dad's job is much the same. He leads and protects. The main purpose of his job is to constantly point his family toward Jesus.

Now Relax!

I can already see that some of you have steam coming out of your ears over this issue of headship. Now relax a minute. Let's look at God's plan found in the Bible. It's found in I Corinthians 11:3; "Now I want you to realize that the head of every man is Christ, and the head of the woman is man, and the head of Christ is God". Then let's add Ephesians 6:1, "Children, obey your parents in the Lord, for this is right."

Picture His plan looking something like this:

```
GOD
CHRIST

MAN

WOMAN

CHILDREN
```

If you will notice, according to Scripture, everyone has someone in headship over them. Even Jesus Christ, who although He was Himself God, submitted willingly to God His Father (John 8:28, John 10:18, John 5:19).

No one was singled out as the doormat or as the unlucky recipient of headship over them. God's plan does not indicate importance or place higher value on one member over another. Each individual under the headship of God is equally important.

Multipurpose Design

First, the whole plan is designed so there is some order in the home. If there is no one in charge or ultimately responsible, there is total chaos. Our God is not a God of confusion.

Second, I believe headship also exists for the purpose of serving each other and building each other up. It requires those in headship to have an attitude of putting the needs of the other person first. Ephesians 5:21 says, "Submit to one another out of reverence for Christ." This is the reason we submit to each other. It is out of our reverence and respect for Christ and His divine plan

Jesus is the perfect example to us of how headship is to work. Even though He was also God. He honored the Father who was the head over Him. He didn't demand independence or equal rights. As He fit under His Father's headship, He also honored and served those under His own headship. This is a perfect example of how men, women and children are to fit into God's perfect plan.

Lastly, I believe headship was designed to offer a system of protection for the family.

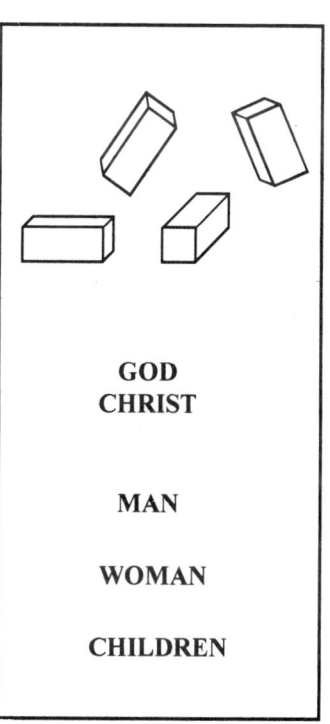

Let's go back to our diagram and demonstrate this system of protection. Let's pretend it's raining bricks:

GOD
CHRIST

MAN

WOMAN

CHILDREN

Now if it's raining bricks -- someone is going to get clobbered, aren't they? Please notice that God has a plan of protection for the family that looks like the diagram below:

Each person under the umbrella is offered God's protective covering. Now, understand what I mean by protection. This does not necessarily mean protection from all physical harm or injury -- but spiritual protection -- offered by being under the covering of God.

Now, in the family, God has asked the man to hold this umbrella of protection (I Corinthians 11:3). It was God's choice. It was part of His plan for the family:

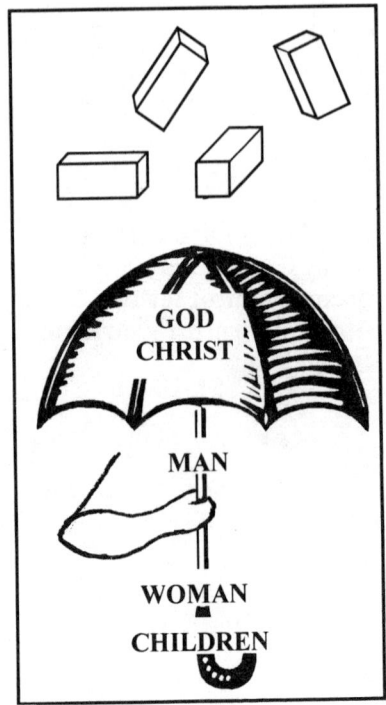

Remember now, man didn't exactly wave his hand in the air and volunteer to hold it. He didn't beg God to let him hold it. He'd probably even say he wasn't really qualified to hold it. Most of the time he would rather have someone else hold it. He's tired after working all day. When he gets home, he'd rather just sink down into that recliner and vegetate rather than be the head of his home and hold that umbrella. However, God has asked the man to be the head of his home. It is his **God-appointed** job. Man didn't choose it. **God did.**

So, this is why we honor Dad as the leader or head of the home. We are honoring the position into which God has placed Dad. It is not tied to performance. Rather, supporting Dad as the head of the home and leader of the family is done out of obedience to God. It is not because Dad necessarily deserves our honor and support but we do it because God asks us to. We do it out of our love for God and our obedience to Him.

What If I Don't Feel Like It?

I don't know about you -- but I don't always feel like honoring someone who isn't doing their part. I don't feel like honoring when I know I could probably do the job just as well as they are. Remember ladies -- this is a feeling! We need to quit 'feeling' and starting obeying what God asks us to do.

That's Impossible

Honor? That's impossible! OK -- maybe not impossible -- but somedays, an unbelievably difficult task. It's difficult enough to know we can't do it on our own or in our own strength. We are going to need to depend on Jesus. He is the only one who can teach us how to honor the position even if the person isn't producing!

Even though He was Himself God, Jesus was asked to honor someone. He was the perfect example. Jesus honored His Father. Well, it wouldn't be so difficult to honor God. After all, He's perfect. He doesn't throw his socks on the floor. He doesn't disappoint you. He's the perfect Father. Of course, it would be easy to honor Him.

Remember, Jesus honored His disciples by washing their feet. They were less than perfect men. They let Him down. They denied Him. They sold Him out. Yet, He chose to honor them. He understands our struggle. It is impossible to do in our own strength. He is the only one who can help us honor a less than perfect Dad.

Why Make It Impossible?

God asked men to lead their families -- to be the head. There are many times when they would rather let someone else do it. So then, why did He give them such an impossible job? He gave them an impossible job so they too must depend on Jesus to get it done. It is meant to be overwhelming and challenging so they will seek Jesus as they strive to lead their families in a Godly way. In this way, if they succeed in leading their families, Jesus gets the credit -- not man. It all depends on Jesus.

What did Jesus ask us as women to do in the family? Genesis 2:18 says, "...it is not good for the man to be alone..." (My husband will say, 'Amen!' to that verse.) To me, it says we were made as a companion for our husbands.

Let's go on with that verse. "I will make a helper suitable for him." I was also made as a helper for him. Helper? Helper! What kind of a second class job is 'helper'! What does that make him -- king?? Oooh, have those words rolled off your tongue? I've chewed them around in my mouth a time or two but Jesus changed my heart. He let me see that being a wife is an honorable job. It isn't second class at all.

Being a helper is **just as important** as being a leader. They are **equally important jobs** -- they just happen to be **different** jobs.

Yes, we operate as partners in our home, with jobs of equal importance. We work together. We honor and respect each other. We talk together before decisions are made but we also understand and accept God's perfect plan for the role we each play in the family unit.

Complementary Jobs

The individual jobs God has given us, complement each other and are necessary in each family for harmony and unity. Looking back to the Scripture in Genesis 2:18, we see that God knew man was lonely and would need a companion. This is what I am to Mike -- his companion.

To me it means I'm not going to let him flounder out there alone as the leader but I'm going to be a true companion. It means I am a faithful supporter as he does his job of trying to head our family. I'm not going to fight him -- but as a true companion -- I will stand by him. As a helper, I will be ready to offer any insight and wisdom when decisions are made. A helper just doesn't stand there. A helper stands with him -- through the good and the bad.

God knew man would need help in leading his family. That is why he asked me to be a helper to Mike. It also says woman would be "a helper *suitable* for him." That means God knew just what Mike would need in a helper and God sent **me**. I was suitable for Mike. I was just what he needed. **No one else** could fill the bill. There is nothing second class about that.

As women, the Bible says we were created as a helper to man. It's one of the most important jobs given to a woman. So, why is it the hardest job for women to do? Come on -- admit it! You know how we are. If our man hesitates even a second -- we're right there ready to grab the baton of leadership.

It's difficult for many of us to help instead of stepping in and leading. I believe God made it this way so that we also will have to depend on Jesus to do our job. So at the end of the day, if we were able to follow and support the leader of our home as a Godly woman, we wouldn't get any credit. It's really an impossible job for us to do. So if we succeed in helping and supporting our husband as the head of our home rather than grabbing leadership -- all the credit goes to Jesus. It is impossible to do without Him.

The Hardest Job for Children?

How about your children? I'm sure your children **always** say, "Yes, Mom -- of course I'll clean my room **and** could I please do the dishes when I'm done?" Sure!! Children don't just naturally love to obey -- do they?

The Bible really only gives children one job assignment. Ephesians 6:1 says, "Children, obey your parents in the Lord, for this is right." This may be the only job they are given but it is also the **most difficult** job for a child. So, like us, they must cry out to Jesus for help. At the end of the day, if they have obeyed their parents as God has commanded, they know the credit goes to Jesus.

You see -- each one of us in the family must depend on Jesus to accomplish the impossible job given us[1]. This is so we realize that Jesus enables us. He is our strength and guide. We can do nothing on our own. We need Jesus in every area of our lives -- especially in our own home.

All Those in Favor

Well, why don't we just take a vote to find out who should do which job in our homes? Some days, I could scrape up enough votes to get elected as leader.

Maybe the person who is the most willing should get the job. I like to lead. I was the head of our home for 16 years. Why not give it back to me? I'd do a great job!

How about passing out the jobs in the home according to qualifications? After all, aren't some women just natural leaders. Isn't it better for them to just take over and lead in those situations where they're better qualified?

I can tell you, if Jesus picked the one most eager to lead in our home -- at the end of the day -- you know who would get the credit. ME! If I led, I would more than likely do it in my own strength and might. **I'd** get the credit! When Mike leads, it is out of obedience to Jesus. He doesn't always love the job or even feel he's qualified. He **knows** he must depend on Jesus to show him how to lead his family. Then, **Jesus** gets the credit!

When I strive to help my husband and to come under his headship -- it isn't because it's the job I do the best or feel most qualified to do. It is done out of my love and obedience to Jesus. I must depend on Jesus to fulfill my role in the family.

It is no different for our son, Matt. When he was living at home, he would probably have loved to be the leader of our home some days but Jesus asked him to obey his parents. It was not his favorite job but the Scripture points out that it was his only job as a child. So when Matt tried to obey his parents, we reminded him the reason he did it was out of his love for and obedience to Jesus (John 14:15).

In our home, there is no dictator -- no slave. We each try to work together with the other family members to fill the

---

[1] Jesus at Home, Lewis F. and Sandra Shaffer, Son Shine Ministries, Int'l, 1981, p92.

role God has given us. We do this because we want our home to be operating according to His plan. Do we always do it perfectly? No -- but we are daily working to follow the example God has given us.

In our homes, we were each given a role specifically designed to cause us to depend on Jesus and not ourselves. Isn't that a great plan! It all points us to Jesus!

Practice - Practice - Practice

One of the best places we get to practice honoring Dad's position is in the area of decision making. Now in our home, Mike and I both discuss the issue before decisions are made. We are a great balance to each other. When one of us disagrees on an item, it may be time to hold the item until later or go back and spend more time in prayer before the decision is made. However, I believe the final decision rests with Mike. I trust him to be seeking God's will and I believe this is part of the headship role Jesus has given him.

As wives, we should definitely offer advice and wise counsel before the decision is made. This can be a great help to our husbands. Do you know what makes our counsel 'wise' counsel? It is wise if we have prayed and asked Jesus if we should share it and how to share it. This makes it wise counsel. James 3:17 says, "But the wisdom that comes from heaven is first of all pure; then peace loving, considerate, submissive, full of mercy and good fruit, impartial and sincere".

Isn't this the type of wise counsel you'd like your husband to receive from you? Ask Jesus when to offer and how to offer counsel to your husband. This allows you be a Godly helper to him -- instead of a sergeant who orders him around or a mother who makes him take action.

What If He Won't Make A Decision?

The reason to take decisions to your husband is to help him assume the role of leader and head of the home[3]. It gives him the opportunity -- the open door to lead. But, what if all you ever hear is: "I don't care." "Do whatever you want." "Umgh!" "You decide." What do you do? Give up?

---

[3] Jesus at Home, Lewis F. and Sandra Shaffer, Son Shine Ministries, Int'l, 1981, p94.

3 5

No -- you are never left alone in the decision making process. If your husband doesn't take the opportunity to lead -- you are not left out there on a limb. Remember your umbrella?

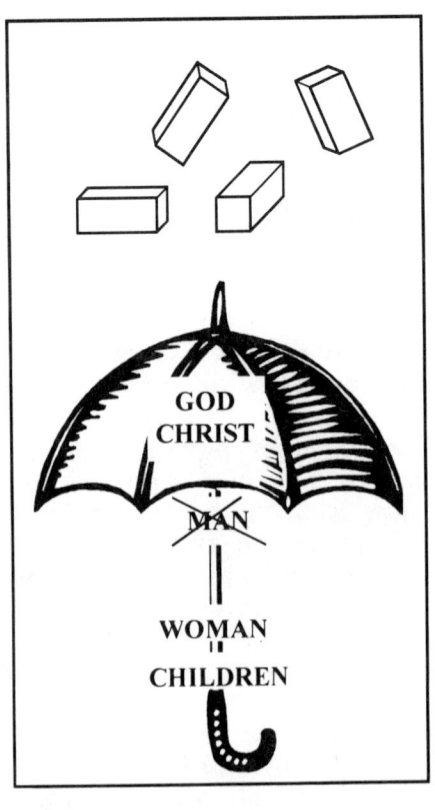

GOD
CHRIST
~~MAN~~
WOMAN
CHILDREN

If you take the husband out of the picture, you still have Jesus to make the decision with you. (Single women -- see how this also applies to you? You are never alone in making decisions either.) Now, once you and Jesus have a decision, you can then take the decision back to your husband and ask him if it's OK with him. See? It still keeps him in the leadership *position.*

Of course, the husband is commanded by God to lead his family but he always has the choice of accepting or refusing the leadership or headship position in his own home. Just make sure you don't automatically take it away. We want our husbands to act like men of God -- and yet we treat them like children. We get in the habit of making all the decisions for them or mocking the ones they finally do make. Open the door for your husband to be the Godly head of your home by taking decisions to him and respecting those decisions he makes.

What If He Doesn't Listen?

So what if you give your wise counsel and he turns right around and decides to do it his own way? You just know his way is going to fail. You are sure his way is the hard way. Shouldn't you go back and counsel again until he listens or at least apply some other sort of pressure, such as pouting or shouting! After all, how does he know what's best?

I Peter 3:1-2, gives some Godly advice in this situation. It says, "Wives, in the same way be submissive to your husbands so that, if any of them do not believe the Word, they may be won over without talk by the behavior of their wives when they see the purity and reverence of your lives." Without talk? Isn't that a tough one! Won over by our behavior? You mean I have to walk not talk! Yes, the Bible says there are times to say and times to pray.

Many of us are afraid to just let go. This is where the 'what-ifs' usually come in. "What if this happens?-- What if he makes a mistake?" We try to second guess the outcome. Some of us even try to fix the outcome. I believe the real issue here is trusting Jesus. How big is Jesus to you? Is He bigger than a mistake?

Is Jesus really bigger than Dad? Sometimes we don't act like it. Sometimes we act as if we don't trust Jesus enough to take our hands off our husbands. Then, who is in charge? It's definitely not Jesus!

There is a wonderful verse in Jeremiah 32:27, "I am the Lord, the God of all mankind. Is anything too hard for me?" Remember this the next time you think you can't let go. Nothing is too hard for Him!

I've Lived It!

I'll never forget one Christmas when Matt was a young teen. It was a lean year financially and we only had a couple of gifts for Matt under the tree. There was a little more money in savings we **could** have spent and I wanted to do just that. I was willing to sacrifice for him. **My** son needed more gifts to open. I didn't want him disappointed on Christmas.

Mike loves Matt very much and wants the best for him, too. He said, "I don't believe we need to buy Matt any more gifts -- this will be enough." I struggled. I even thought of going behind his back and buying just a couple more 'small' things so Matt would have more under the tree. Mike listened to my points openly but still knew buying more gifts was not the answer. When he didn't change his decision, I applied more pressure, hoping he would finally give in. I even resorted to a short 'pouting party'. I finally gritted my teeth and accepted that this would be the **worst** Christmas in our entire family history -- thanks to Dad!

Christmas came and packages were opened. I felt such a sadness as Matt opened only a couple of things from us. When we were cleaning up the wrapping paper, I said, "Matt, I'm really sorry we didn't have many things under the tree for you this year." Matt just looked at me and said, "Mom, look how much I got this Christmas. A couple of days ago, Aunt Betty gave me their extra color TV for my room and just before Christmas I got Grandma's car to drive. I got a lot, Mom." Through Mike's decision (which looked like an A-#1 blooper to me) God had given Matt the opportunity to recall all he had received instead of looking at all he didn't.

Many times, when Dad makes a decision with which we don't agree -- we are afraid of the results. We panic and just step right in and interfere. We try to fix it! We virtually yank the umbrella out of his hand and say we can do it better. I wanted to shower our son with gifts. I wanted to fix the whole situation and make Matt feel better. If I would have stepped in and yanked the umbrella from Mike's hands, I would have short-changed Matt from learning a very valuable spiritual lesson. In addition, I would have probably earned disrespect from my husband.

Trust God's plan for the family. He created it and He knows it can work.

Who's in Charge Here?

Now, I want to ask you a few questions. Did you have to stay awake last night to make sure your heart kept beating? No? It beat without your help! Did you have to hold your bed down so it wouldn't float away? No? Oh, you say gravity kept it down. Any stars fall out of the sky and klunk you on the head today? No? They stayed in the sky without your help? How is that possible?

Let's take a look at Psalm 104. Verse 5-7 says, "He set the earth on its foundations; it can never be moved. You covered it with the deep as with a garment; the waters stood above the mountains. But at your rebuke the waters fled, at the sound of your thunder they took to flight..." It looks as if God is extremely powerful -- in order to be able to set the earth where He wanted it and to get all the waters to go where He wanted them to go.

Then in verse 14 we read: "He makes grass grow for the cattle, and plants for man to cultivate -- bringing forth food from the earth." We don't make things grow. God does. We're just there to cultivate them once God grows them.

God thought of everything! He is powerful enough to accomplish all of that without our help -- isn't He?! Wouldn't you say that He's in charge of the universe? Then, why don't we act as if He's in charge of our lives and homes as well?

Every time we step in and try to rescue -- we're saying: " I know you can hold the stars in the sky, Lord. I know you created everything I see. I know you're in charge of the universe but I just don't trust you to take care of this thing in my life!" That's the case when we jump in if Dad doesn't do it fast enough or jump in if Dad does it wrong (which often means he did it differently than we would have done it). When we jump into situations without praying or before asking Jesus if we are to even step in -- what we're really saying is "I don't trust you, Jesus."

Believe me, even in the most urgent circumstances, there is time to pray and ask Jesus if you are to be the rescue. The problem we get into is we become perpetual rescuers (fixers) -- never giving our family the chance to see Jesus is their Rescuer and not us.

Our Actions Send a Message

Stepping in to rescue not only says we don't trust Jesus, it also sends a message to our children that says, "Dad isn't really the best Dad in the whole world. He just can't do anything right so we have to do it for him. Mom has to do everything over that Dad does."

Ladies, are we afraid of the consequences of Dad's actions? Are we afraid of being embarrassed by Dad? It's true. You or your children may be embarrassed by something Dad does. You may pay a price for a bad decision Dad makes. However, if God can hold the universe together, I believe He can be trusted with our lives. The last time I looked, He was still on the throne. Is He still on the throne of your life or have you taken on the crown yourself?

The Ultimate Test

I know a woman who probably wanted to yank that old umbrella out of her husband's hand! I'm sure she even wondered if God knew what He was doing. Her name was Sarah. To give you a little background -- Sarah and Abraham were promised that many nations would come from them. They waited and waited and waited until finally their son, Isaac, arrived when she was approximately 90 years old. Read Genesis 22 to see what kind of dilemma she faced when she saw Abraham take her only, long awaited child up to the mountain to offer sacrifices.

The Biblical account doesn't say much about Sarah the day of the sacrifice but I believe she knew what was about to happen. She must have eventually realized something wasn't right that morning. She had seen Abraham leave many times to go to the mountain to offer a sacrifice. This time he took Isaac and plenty of wood on the donkey but no sacrificial lamb went with them.

Once she realized what could happen and the possible danger for Isaac, she could have cried, begged and screamed -- "No, not **my** son! There's no way he's risking my son's life. Sacrifice our son -- what kind of father is he! Doesn't he love his son? I'm going after them and bring my Isaac back."

Now, by making this request of Abraham and Sarah, God was calling for a spiritual sacrifice. Would they trust in what they knew rather than what they felt? Sarah surely felt like chasing after them but she waited. The trip up to the mountain normally took three days plus three days for the return trip. So, for a total of six days she waited and waited for Abraham to return. It must have virtually torn her apart emotionally to think she may never see her son again. Maybe after some personal struggle and turmoil, she finally said by her actions, "God, I trust you -- even with my son."

Can you trust Jesus to lead through your husband? Can you trust Jesus with your children? Can you trust Jesus in every area of your life?

What Does That Have To Do With Me?

I believe how we treat Dad affects how we feel as a Mom. It has everything to do with us. Remember in Genesis 2:24, "For this reason a man will leave his father and mother and be united to his wife, and they will become one flesh." Don't ask me to explain how this happens -- but God's Word says the two of us will become one when we marry. If you are married, you and your husband are one. If what you do or say is critical, degrading or destructive towards your husband, it will also affect you because the Bible says you are one with him. What you do and say to your husband should be uplifting because it will ultimately uplift you. He is not your enemy. He is one with you. If you lift him up -- you are lifting up and building up a part of you.

Dad Doesn't Live Here Anymore

If you are a single Mom due to a divorce, I'd like to encourage you with some special words. These words apply even if you are no longer married to the father of your children. These words apply even if he doesn't act like much of a father to your children. Jesus would still have you honor Dad in front of the children. No matter how he has acted towards you or the children -- he is still the father.

I believe Jesus would still have you honor the 'position' of Dad in that child's life. Why? Because Jesus asks you to. In John 14:15 it says, "If you love me you will obey what I command." If you love Jesus -- you'll do what He asks. It's a matter of obedience that flows out of love.

Jesus also commands our children to honor their parents (Exodus 20:12 - one of the 10 Commandments). So Mom, when you honor Dad, it teaches your children to honor Dad, too. Through your example, you are helping them do what Jesus requires of them. I believe it is also important because you are helping your children to form their image of a father in their lives. That will affect sons in how they are learning to father their own children. That will affect most children in how they picture God, their Heavenly Father.

Does this mean you make up lies or try to make Dad look good. No -- ask Jesus how to talk to the children about their Dad. Ask Jesus to make sure all bitterness towards their Dad is gone from your heart or it will surface in your voice and words. (Remember the way to get rid of bitterness is through forgiveness.)

Matthew 12:34b says, "...For out of the overflow of the heart the mouth speaks". In other words, whatever is in your heart will eventually overflow until it pops out of your mouth. If you still hold resentment in your heart,

4 1

resentment will eventually come out of your mouth in the words you speak. If there is joy in your heart, this is what will come out of your mouth. If there is true forgiveness -- this is what your mouth will speak.

The place to begin is in your heart. Once you heart is right, then ask Jesus what positive attributes Dad has and concentrate on those, rather than his weaknesses. Soon, this is what will begin to come out of your mouth.

Strengthening Your Children

Be careful how you say, "You're just like your Dad!". It's usually not meant as a compliment but rather as a criticism of their Dad and therefore a criticism of them. Do you want to strengthen your children? Then point out the good things in their Dad. They will identify and associate with what you think and say about their Dad -- because they are a part of him. Did you hear me? They are part of their Dad and this fact can never be changed. So, please -- help to strengthen your children by respecting their Dad and speaking respectfully about him.

Building Future Moms and Dads

I'm sure we'd all agree we want our sons to grow up to be great Dads. So if you have a son, help him get a healthy picture of fatherhood. This will help even if his own Dad wasn't the best example of a healthy, caring Dad. Read to him about Dads in the Bible. Don't compare the Dads in the Bible to his Dad but read it to give him Godly examples to follow. Remember even Dads in the Bible made mistakes. Help him to see Dads aren't perfect so when he becomes a Dad, he will know if he trusts in Jesus, perfection is not expected. Jesus will help him be all that he needs to be for his own children, even if his earthly father wasn't the perfect example to follow.

If you have a daughter, I'm sure you would agree you want her to be a great Mom when she grows up. Do you want her to have a healthy picture of motherhood? If you do, then show her what the Bible says about honoring Dad. Speaking kindly to her about Dad helps her to do the same. She too, must see that even if her own Dad let her down, God, her Heavenly Father, will never leave or forsake her.

Psalms 68:5 says, He will be "a father to the fatherless..."
Even when her Dad wasn't all she needed, God was her
Father and was all she ever needed. If your daughter never
even knew her Dad, she never lacked a Father. Knowing
this will build her womanhood on the foundation of Jesus
Christ -- not on a frail human being.

I know the hurts of divorce are very deep but please Mom,
make sure you have forgiven past hurts so your children are
also free to forgive Dad. Remind them to pray for their Dad.
You can be the example of forgiveness by praying with them
for their Dad.

If you're tempted to say, "I can't forgive him." --
remember Philippians 4:13 which says, "I can do everything
through Him (Jesus) who gives me strength." Don't try to
forgive in your own strength. Ask Jesus for the strength to
forgive.

Honoring Dad Even Behind His Back?

Oh -- haven't we all been tempted with things like:
"Now don't tell Dad we're doing this...."
"I know Dad doesn't want you to do this --
but just this once I'll let you...."
"Here's $5 -- don't breathe a word to Dad.
He'll be mad!"
We can honor Dad to his face all day long -- but what we
say behind his back is the true test of honoring. If we say
things like those above, it says to our children that Dad's
standards, rules and decisions are wrong. It says he isn't
really smart or very good at being a Dad, so we'll just go
around him. It dishonors Dad and teaches our children to
disobey Dad if they don't like his rules. It also allows the
children to divide Mom and Dad when they should be
standing as one.

Don't blame the children on this one, Mom. You are the
one who can stop and remind them: "I know this might be
hard but Dad and I are going to stand together on this."

As in my home, I'm sure there are times when Dad does
something to make the kids mad. They run to complain,
"Dad is so mean. He won't let me go to Jim's house tonight!"
What do you say? "I know, Honey. Dad doesn't have any
idea how important it is to you. I can't believe he said no!
You just go and I'll take care of Dad."

43

What we should say is: "Honey, Dad is really trying to do what he thinks is best. You need to do what Dad says. Come on -- it'll work out."

Stand By Your Man

Now, there may be situations when you just can't believe the decision Dad has made. You **know** what's going to happen if you let his decision stand -- soooo, the temptation is to just dive in there and 'rescue' the entire family from destruction. It's happened to me!

One day when Matt was in the sixth grade, he woke up with his entire left eye swollen and reddened. I nearly panicked. I wanted to keep him home from school and take him to the doctor. Mike took my advice into account, but as he prayed, he knew the answer was to send Matt to school.

Whew! That was a tough one! I was a nurse. I knew all the complications that could take place with his eye. He was born with an extensive birthmark near that eye. He had numerous reconstructive operations from the time he was five years old.

Yet, Mike said he knew (through prayer) we were supposed to just bandage his eye and send him to school that day. He assured me the school would call us if there were any further problems. I prayed and prayed that morning as I taped the bandage onto his eye. I wanted to panic and step in and stop the mistake. As I prayed, I knew Jesus was telling me to just relax and let go.

The day dragged by until finally I heard the school bus approach. As I ran to meet the bus, off came Matt, running as fast as his legs could carry him. I could see from a distance the patch was missing from his eye. Before he got close enough for me to see his eye very clearly, I called to asked him where his patch was. He hollered, "It's in my pocket, Mom!" (Oh great! The patch was to keep out infection.) As he got closer I could see his eye was totally normal. The redness and swelling was completely gone.

I learned a new thing about trust. Not just trusting my husband but also about trusting Jesus to care for our son. I also learned how important it was for me to stand with Mike and support his decisions. Can you imagine how Matt would have felt, if instead he had heard me argue with Mike over the decision to send him to school. Matt was like any child who loved a day off from school now and then. He could have used our division as a tool to pressure us into letting him stay home. He might have thought he was sicker than he really was if he had seen me panic. Instead he only saw Mom and Dad stand together. Matt left for school that morning, knowing he could trust Mom and Dad to work together to do the best for him. He learned he could trust Jesus, as well.

You might be thinking, "Hey, that wasn't such a major ordeal. I would have survived that one without panicking and stepping in!" You're probably right. Let me share an even more graphic example of the importance of standing by your man in a united front.

This Was a Biggie !

Matt has always been a great child with a pretty easy going personality. That seemed to change when he was a senior in high school, going through the hormone laden turmoil of a normal male teen. He was struggling with his desire for independence. He thought his parents were the only thing keeping him from being a 'free man'. We became the enemy. He was angry at us and blamed us for ruining his life. He tried making rebellious behavior and disrespectful language a part of his daily existence.

It seemed every day in our home was a battle of some sort. This time I was about to meet the biggest test of standing with my man.

In many areas, Jesus had been working in our hearts to let go of Matt, giving fewer restrictions and more freedoms. Of course, we always encouraged him to pray and seek God's guidance when he made his own choices.

There were also some expectations Matt needed to fulfill if he was to live in our home. After all, we were still the parents and we were not abdicating our position in Matt's life just because he was 18 years old. We were giving him some room to grow but we also had to maintain God's standards of living for our family. Those few restrictions left in his life were exactly what Matt was fighting.

One of the standards for our home was that even as an older teen, Matt was to attend church on Sunday mornings. We highly encouraged but did not require him to attend other weekly services or programs. He was required to attend church -- period. Jesus showed us this was important in the training and upbringing of our son (Proverbs 22:6).

He Tested the Waters

One Sunday morning, Matt came out of his room still in his jogging pants. Mike said, "Son, better hurry up and get ready for church or we'll be late." "I'm not going today, Dad." "What do you mean you're not going, Matt? This is something Jesus has said is important for you and is expected while you live here at home." "Well, I'm not going, Dad!"

After several minutes of unfruitful battle, Mike finally said, "Matt, we love you very much and want you to stay and live with us here in our home but if you can't live with the rules Jesus has asked us as parents to set up -- then, you must leave."

I bit my lip so hard I thought I was going to die. This was my **only** son! He had a car sitting out in the driveway! There was nothing stopping him from getting in the car and driving right out of our lives! Maybe forever!

I didn't say a word in front of Matt but I quietly asked Mike if we could talk in the bedroom a minute. I was a second away from sheer panic! Once we got into the bedroom, I blurted out, "Mike, do you realize he could leave and never come back?" Mike replied, "Yes, Connie -- but he must choose. If he chooses to live here -- he must learn to live under the standards Jesus has asked us to set for him. If he cannot live with those rules, he is free to leave."

My heart was aching and my head pounding but yet, I knew it was true. Mike and I had agreed on this issue many times before. Today, Matt would have to choose whom he would follow. He would choose between his desire to be independent (of his parents and of God) or to follow God's plan for his life by honoring his parents. I knew I, too, must choose -- to be independent (of my husband and of God) and do it my way or to follow God's plan for our family by standing by my husband.

We went back into the kitchen where Matt was sitting at the table. Mike said, "Matt, we love you very much. We want you to stay here and live in our home. If you cannot follow the guidelines and rules Jesus has given us for our family, you must leave. You need to decide. Mom and I are going in to finish getting ready for church and when we come out, we will need to have your decision."

46

Matt started to cry, "Don't make me choose, Dad! Don't make me choose!" Mike said, "Son, you will have to make choices every day of your life. Today you will have to choose to live here or to leave."

As we dressed in the bedroom, we could hear Matt crying at the kitchen table. It almost broke my heart. I found myself biting my lip and holding my hands from reaching for the door knob. Soon the crying stopped. When we came out of the bedroom, Matt was dressed for church. He had decided he would live in our home. We made sure he understood he would be expected to live within the standards set up in our home as we also tried to allow him room to grow.

I am so proud of Matt. I know it was difficult for him that day to back down from his stand and humble himself. I am so proud of Mike for being a Dad who loved his son enough to take a stand, for Jesus sake, and not back down.

Never Stand Between Dad and the Children

That day could have caused not only a great division between parent and child but also between Mom and Dad. If I had stood my ground and acted on my fear that Matt might leave home, I would have divided our home. Mom, please never stand between Dad and the children. Talk to Dad. Share with him any wisdom Jesus has given you about the situation but please, stand beside him -- never against him. Stand beside Dad even when circumstances 'look' all wrong? Yes, even this is possible because we have a God that is bigger than circumstances and situations.

In our case, the situation turned out great. Our son chose to stay and live in our home. It didn't solve every problem in his adolescent life. It didn't instantly turn him into a totally obedient, respectful teenager. What it did do was cause him to know without a doubt, he wasn't calling the shots -- he was not in charge. He wasn't dividing Mom and Dad. We were still the parents, standing together. If he wished to live in our home, he would have to be willing to live with the standards we set. I believe his love, and especially his respect for us as parents, increased that day.

Mark 3:25 says, "If a house is divided against itself, that house cannot stand." How thankful I am; our house stands together.

Why Not Negotiate?

Some of you might be wondering why we just didn't negotiate or let up on some of the standards. I mean, is going to church **really** that important if he wasn't even going with the right attitude? Was it important enough to possibly cause our son to leave in anger? Going to church wasn't the real issue here -- it could have been any issue that caused his early morning rebellion. The real issue was our headship over him as parents.

Many parents today are listening to the popular advice of psychologists and child care specialists. They are trying to negotiate with their children. I want you to remember that no where in the Scripture does it say, 'parents negotiate with your children'. It says in Proverbs 22:6, "Train a child in the way he should go". As parents we need to take that responsibility seriously. We may not always be popular with our children. We may at times feel like the only parents in the world doing it God's way. Stand strong and believe that God's Word is true!

In addition, we don't negotiate because any standard is important if Jesus says it is important. We do listen to our child but we don't just automatically change things to keep peace. If Jesus says it's important -- we will stand firm. Ask Jesus what standards are important for your children and then be willing to carry them out with His love.

What If the Story Had Ended Differently?

What if he **had** walked out the door that day. Then what? As hard as it is for me to say, I would still have to stand by Dad. Our son took a great step in his own personal growth that day. He had to stand up and make a difficult choice. If he chose to walk out -- he would then have to live with the consequences of his choice. If he chose to stay -- he would have to live with the limits the choice brought with it. The choice was his!

Standing by Dad doesn't mean you are ganging up on your children -- two against one. It means you are uniting in your decisions and support each other in those decisions. Stand by your man! It will bless your children. It will also bless you.

No Criticizing or Complaining

Sometimes Dads can get angry or react out of frustration (or simply put -- 'blow a gasket'). This can and does happen in most normal homes. Dads are human, too. If this does happen, can you just hug your child and say, "It's going to be all right."?   Can you say it without criticizing or complaining about Dad behind his back?

Philippians 4:8 says, "....whatever is true, whatever is noble, whatever is right, whatever is pure, whatever is lovely, whatever is admirable -- if anything is excellent or praiseworthy - think about such things." Remember ladies, whatever is in your heart will eventually come popping out of your mouth. So why not fill your heart (your thoughts) with whatever is pure and praiseworthy. Then, those things pure and praiseworthy will come out of your mouth as you speak.

While smart remarks like "Men have no brains!" or "Who died and made him king?" may make you feel better -- they only serve to make children feel as if their Dad is incompetent. They may even feel as if their Dad is the worst Dad in the whole world. They won't want to honor a man you don't respect or honor. When we build up Dad in front of the children, this is what they will begin to think about Dad.

The Bible says, "Train a child in the way he should go..." Mom, are you training your children to respect Dad? Are you speaking well of Dad to the children? Are you honoring him so they see a living example of how Jesus expects them to honor Dad?

Remember, if you are married, you are one with your husband. So, if you build up Dad, you will be building up Mom at the same time. In the process, you will be building up your whole family.

If you are a single mom -- tearing down Dad will not serve any purpose but to harbor the anger or guilt and make it grow.   Remember, this principle also implies if I tear down Dad - I am actually tearing myself down as well as the fiber of my whole family.

It's Never Too Late

I want to be the best Mom in the whole world - so then why do I feel like the worst? Could it be because I treat Dad like the worst Dad in the whole world?   Today you can begin to honor the **position** Jesus has given Dad. It will also honor Jesus and bless your family. It's **never** too late to change.

Let's make this our daily prayer:

Father, You see us everyday. You know how our home operates and it's not always peaceful and in order. Help me to remember Your ways are perfect. Help me to honor and respect Dad so my children will learn by my example. Most of all, I want them to see me love and honor You with all I do.

In Jesus' name,
Amen.

Take time to think about these questions:

1. If I were to make a diagram of our family (see page 28), what would it look like?

2. Is there ever a battle for control in our family? Who usually wins?

3. On a scale of 1-10, how would I rate myself in 'standing by my man'?

4. What step can I personally take to help our family better follow God's plan?

4

I Want to be the Best Mom in the World - So Then Why Do I Feel Like the Worst ??....

Because My Child Has Disappointed Me !!

From the minute I found out I was pregnant, I began to envision what our child would be like. He would be perfect. He would always clean his room -- not be messy like some other people's children. He would always be polite -- not rude like some other people's children. He would be the smartest child around -- not like some other people's children. He would never disappoint me -- not like some other people's children. He would be all I wanted him to be.

Once Matt was born, these visions got even clearer and stronger. You might call them expectations. I expected Matt to act a certain way and when he didn't, I was disappointed. Haven't we all been there? Disappointed because of something our children did or didn't do?

A Nation of Child Watchers

In America, it seems we are intense child watchers. We watch every step of our child's growth and development with a magnifying glass. We compare our child's progress to national averages, to charts, to their siblings or to any other child around who looks as if they are close to their age. We rate their growth and progress and when it somehow doesn't match up -- we're disappointed. If little Susie doesn't walk as soon as little Johnny does -- we're disappointed. We want our children to be the best, the most, the fastest, the smartest. We even rate their popularity. When our children aren't invited to a birthday party and everyone else is -- we're disappointed. When they grow up and decide to throw away some of our values -- we're disappointed.

They Are a Part of Us

Disappointment can bring feelings of rejection or inferiority to us as parents. As Moms, we especially seem to identify closely with our children. They are a part of us. If they are rejected or just don't match up to other kids -- it feels as if we are being rejected and don't match up either. If our children reject our values and or won't accept our advice -- we take it personally. It feels as if they are rejecting us and everything for which we stand. It is because they are a part of us that we take this hurt and disappointment so deeply and personally.

Little Issues Make Big Disappointments

I think both you and I know it's not always the big stuff that causes the biggest disappointments. For me, it was the little issue of clothes -- the way Matt dressed. When he was a toddler, he was such a cute, blond-headed, pudgy little guy. I loved to dress him up and show him off. He was without a doubt, the cutest child ever created.

When Matt started school, he wanted to dress himself. I expected things to match. He didn't necessarily care if they matched. He was just happy to get them on frontwards instead of backwards -- and sometimes that didn't even matter. To him, cars, trucks, toys and friends were far more important than how he dressed. Day after day, I sent him back to his room to change clothes because they didn't match. When I sent him back to his room to change clothes, my actions said I was disappointed in his choices. Sometimes I would beat him to the punch and go in and pick out the matching clothes to avoid the conflict.

The little issue of clothes caused a huge disappointment in my life. He didn't match up to the picture of the perfect child I had created in my head. I'm sure it caused disappointment in Matt's life, too. He knew he had to dress a certain way to get his Mom's approval. He could see the disappointment in my face and hear it in my voice each time he didn't match up to my expectations. Many times, with my actions, I said clothes were more important than he was.

Difference Between Guiding and Controlling

When our children are very young, we make the choices for them. By watching us, they also learn how to make choices. As they get a little older, they still need some guidance in getting dressed and ready for school. In my case, I could have let Matt pick from two or three outfits. He would still learn how to make choices in his life but with some guidelines. Guiding our children is one method of teaching and training them in the decision making process. As they get older, we widen their window of choices.

In this area, my problem was I didn't stop at guiding and training. I let it become control. I had expectations and if they weren't met, I took over. I became a controller. I couldn't stand being disappointed by his clothing choices every day, so when he was young, I made all the choices for him.

As he got older, he still didn't care much about clothes. Friends, computers, his car...those were important to him. How he dressed just didn't seem to matter to him. It did to me! I thought how he dressed reflected on my competency as a Mom. Others would look at our son and say, "He must have a great Mom. Look at how nicely he always looks."

I had expectations that he would grow up and dress in the preppy style so popular in the 90's. You know -- polo shirts, sweaters and casual pants. No way! He thought T-shirt and jeans were fine. It didn't even matter if the T-shirt looked as if it had been squashed for a week or two by the local, friendly elephant. (By the way, T-shirts and jeans were fine but I didn't want to let go of my expectations.)

Why wouldn't he just dress the way I wanted him to? He would have looked so great! The girls would have noticed him! When he was an older teen, I couldn't just storm into his room and pull out what he'd wear for the day as I had done when he was young. So I started suggesting. "Why don't you wear the great looking shirt your Grandma bought you for Christmas? You look so good in blue." When that didn't work, I started nagging. (You know what nagging is. It's suggesting it more than once and the tone of your voice begins to take on a different quality.)

When I got desperate, it began to sound like..."I can't believe you're wearing that shirt again today! Don't you have any other clothes in your closet? Those jeans?...Over my dead body!"

The Results?

I found when we let guiding become controlling, one of two things can happen in older children. Depending on their personality, they will usually rebel or give in. If the choice is rebellion, it could be an out and out battle over who is in control or it could surface subtly in another issue of independence.

If they give in, emotions may be turned inward. There may be the desire to rebel and call for independence but the risk may be too high to take. Constant expressions of disappointment can make children feel as if they aren't worthy or good enough. To them it may sound like this: "If Mom's always disappointed in me -- it must mean I'm always doing something wrong. I must be bad. I must be dumb." In a teenager's head it may sound like this..."I can never do it right! It's never good enough for her anyway -- so I'll just quit trying!"

Our Day Arrived

Our son, Matt, was the cutest little toddler you ever saw in your whole life! He had beautiful, thick, blond hair and dimples that could charm your socks right off your feet! His pudgy little arms and legs were so precious. You just couldn't help hugging him. He was such an agreeable, compliant child. (In other words, he did it my way and rarely fought City Hall.)

That is, until he grew up a little and decided he wanted to take control of his own hair. Our day had arrived! I would now get to practice trusting Jesus in a new way.

Mom - I Want a 'Marine Buzz'

Our seven year old came home one day and announced he wanted a 'Marine buzz'. That was the 'shaved to the scalp' look found on any new military recruit. Now remember -- we're talking about 1980. No one -- and I mean no one, was having their hair cut that way! Matt discussed

5 4

it with his Dad and they thought it was a cool idea. I was devastated.

As Mike and I talked it over, I couldn't come up with a good reason not to let him cut his hair. We agreed the only thing we felt absolutely essential concerning hair was it always had to be kept clean and neat. Reluctantly, I had to agree.

So, Dad set up the video camera, took out the clippers and did the honors himself. As I saw his beautiful hair fall away from his head in clumps, I realized I was so against the shaven look because no one else was doing it. I was afraid he would be ostracized. I wanted everyone to like our son. I didn't want him to be different.

He went to school the next day knowing some kids might make fun of him. He really didn't seem to care. He wanted a 'Marine buzz' and even potential rejection by his friends -- would not dissuade him. I have to respect Matt for making choices that were not based on peer pressure.

As a postscript -- by the end of the next week nearly every boy in his class was sporting that same new recruit look. Matt made a choice and didn't fear the consequences. It was a choice we could allow (even if I did it reluctantly). My disappointment in his choice of hair style had nothing to do with hair but everything to do with my expectations being met.

I Must Be a Slow Learner

You would think this one event would be enough to cure me from the hair phobia but I must be a slow learner. He outgrew the bald look and cruised through much of the teen years with fairly normal looking hair. When Matt was about 17 years old, we were about to embark on another round of 'hair mania' when he decided to grow his hair all one length. (You know -- the hippie look!) I'm not even sure disappointed is a strong enough word to describe my feelings! How about livid! ("How could he!! What will other people think!") How about explosive! ("He's just doing this to make me mad! He knows long hair bugs me!")

Our clean cut son now looked as if he could be a resident of some hippie commune. What was so difficult about keeping his hair short? Was that too much to ask? I was disappointed. He didn't look like I thought he should look. He didn't meet my expectations.

Of course, if I would have just waited long enough, I would have seen the style change again when he entered the military after high school. He once again sported a 'buzz'. (Doesn't God have a sense of humor!)

Choose Your Battles Wisely

I remember watching a film series about teens. The speaker said, "You need to choose your battles." In our home, I tried to make everything that fell short of my desires a battle. It meant Matt and I battled over everything. I wanted him to become a miniature Connie. Jesus wanted Matt to become Matt. He needed the freedom to become all Jesus had created him to be -- not a miniature model of his Mom. In my heart, that's what I really wanted for Matt, too. I just wasn't sure how to make it happen.

Some of the issues in our home, were battles chosen with my emotions and feelings. Battles chosen wisely are those chosen in prayer. When our children choose to disobey and go against those prayerful standards, they are not just disappointing us, they are also disappointing Jesus.

Once they begin to understand the sincerity with which you carry out God's standards for your family, you will be helping them to understand how serious God is about their well being. It is not just parents making rules. It is parents who are seeking God's guidance (praying) for their children. It is parents who are then seeking God's strength to carry out those standards.

Two Mottos for Life

I am an extremely intense individual. I take things very seriously -- including rules and guidelines. With my intense personality, it's easy for me to become the drill sergeant of our family. Our son went to Army bootcamp. He can tell you first hand, the drill sergeant wasn't always the most pleasant person in his day.

I can say, with my whole heart, I didn't want to be the drill sergeant parent. I wanted to be the kind of parent who guided my child but also wasn't afraid to stand firm when God said it was an important issue.

However, I also wanted to be the kind of parent who wasn't so rigid that discipline was more important than love. Now, discipline is important. Without it, our children grow up unable to control their actions and lack self discipline in many areas of their lives. Discipline is an important part of guiding our children but is it more important than love in your home? If it is, your home will be filled with more rules than love. It will be run by a drill sergeant rather than by the loving arms of a parent.

To keep love more important than discipline, I personally had to learn a couple of little mottos:

DON'T SWEAT THE SMALL STUFF

This phrase reminds me that when it comes to worry, it's only big enough if Jesus says it's big enough. Everything else is small stuff and I don't have to worry about it.

When I am anxious, frightened or angry with my son, I am reminded of the second motto:

WHEN I GET TO HEAVEN, WILL THIS REALLY MATTER?

If the answer to this question is 'yes' -- I can continue to be anxious, frightened or angry. If the answer is 'no' -- I can relax, ask Jesus how to handle it and trust Him with the results.

These two mottos are reminders that help me put every day earthly issues into a heavenly perspective.

Learning to Take Responsibility for Their Actions

When Matt got his driver's license, we told him that if he got a speeding ticket or some other driving infraction, he would lose his driving privileges. Accidents could happen but we felt strongly there was no excuse for speeding or breaking the law. When he came home with a speeding ticket, my first response was to jump all over him and take his license away immediately. We'd discuss reinstatement when he was thirty years old and finally responsible. How could he do this to us? People would see it in the newspaper and see our child had broken the law. I was disappointed.

Mike reminded me Matt told us about the ticket immediately, with no excuses. He accepted responsibility for his actions. At that point, Jesus made it clear we needed to be thankful Matt told us and didn't try to cover it up. He didn't try to blame it on someone or something else. He accepted full financial responsibility for the ticket. He told us -- knowing he stood the chance of losing his driving privileges and an increase in insurance rates which would be at his expense. He was not a terrible kid. He was a young man learning to take responsibility for his actions.

Jesus showed us in this case, his honesty was more important than the punishment he might receive. Yes, he did have to pay higher insurance rates and still was paying almost five years later. There was a cost for disobedience he had to pay. The greater lesson was learning to accept responsibility for his actions.

He has never had another speeding ticket and is an extremely responsible driver. I tend to believe learning to take responsibility for his actions was an influencing factor in this area of his life.

Separate the Sin from the Sinner

That night, feelings of disappointment could have been so strong they would have become much more important than Matthew. I could have made him pay a much higher price than the price of a speeding ticket and increased insurance rates. If the disappointment I felt was allowed to rule rather than Jesus, disappointment would have dictated Matt's punishment. I would have held him emotional hostage until my disappointment began to decrease. I had done it before. Every time I did, I was sending the message to Matt I was disappointed in who he was.

That night, Jesus made it very clear I needed to separate Matt from the event. It was all right to be disappointed when he made a wrong choice. That disappointment was the sadness I felt over sin. Jesus also feels sadness over sin but He separates the sin from the sinner. He always hated the sin but loved the sinner. I needed to be able to do this, too. When Matt makes wrong choices -- I need to hate the sin (the act he had committed) but still love him unconditionally.

Men React Differently

As a Mom, do you know how difficult that is to do? Women, by nature, seem to integrate people, events, places and feelings. We tie everything together. It's all interrelated. My husband, Mike, can separate feelings from actions much more easily than I can. Men seem to be able to put things away in little drawers or compartments. They are able to separate themselves from the emotional impact of the event more quickly than women. It's the way most men are made.

I remember when Matt was about eight years old. We were invited to a friend's house for dinner. We had a great time and Matt always enjoyed playing with their children. The next day, I got a call asking if Matt had taken a particular item from her husband's collection at their home. Matt said he hadn't. Then, on a Saturday morning several weeks later, Matt and I were in his room doing a 'major overhaul' of his toy box. As we sorted and cleaned, I picked up a toy that was new to me. My stomach began to churn as I asked Matt if he had taken it from their house. He admitted he did.

At first, I was so angry that screaming instantly seemed like the natural thing to do. Then my reaction quickly turned to disappointment. I felt as if my heart would break in two. I was disappointed he had stolen the item and even more disappointed he lied to me about it. It was a double whammy. What kind of parents were we? Hadn't we taught him any better? We were Christians. Christians don't steal. Christians don't lie. Hadn't we raised him right? Then, I was disappointed because he made me look bad in front of our friends! Didn't he care how he made us look? Didn't he love Jesus? Didn't he love us?

Mike was on a temporary military assignment away from home so I knew I had to handle this immediately rather than wait for him to come home in several weeks. I called our friends and asked if we could come over. I made Matt confess to what he'd done and ask for forgiveness. This guy was wonderful. He took Matt into another room and talked to him. He told him it was a sin to steal and that disappointed Jesus. He also told Matt Jesus forgave him and so did he.

I watched over a period of months and the relationship between this man and Matt seemed to remain the same.

59

Their relationship never really deteriorated. He seemed to be able to separate Matt from the incident with very little difficulty. He never made us feel Matt wasn't welcome in their home. It was forgiven and forgotten.

Not As Easy for Women

I'm not so sure it was as easy for his wife to put the incident behind. Some of her reaction may have had to do with personality differences but I believe it also stemmed from the general differences between a man and a woman. They differ in their ability to separate things -- to put them away in a box. Once the incident was over, the husband put it in a little drawer.

As women, we sometimes keep all of our little incidents and events folded neatly on top of the dresser. They are easily visible and an ever present reminder of what took place. In Matt's case. this might be what the wife did because the relationship between she and Matt was always a little strained after that. It was as if she seemed to be keeping a close eye on him; just waiting to see if he would do something else.

It's not that she didn't want to forget and let go. It was just more difficult for her to separate the incident and put it aside.

Don't Take It Personally

Ladies, we tend to take everything that happens to those we love very personally. We take it as a personal affront. We perceive it as a personal attack. We feel as if our hearts are the target when others disappoint us. I beat myself up and threw myself on the ground as I took blame and shame for what happened that day.

I want to remind you our children make personal choices. Just as He gave Adam and Eve the freedom to make choices, God also gives our children the freedom to choose right from wrong. When they choose to sin -- it is a personal issue between them and God. Yes, we are responsible as parents to aim them back to Jesus when they sin. This is where they will find repentance and forgiveness. We also must be able to separate ourselves and not take it personally. Do you know the only way we can do this is to ask Jesus to help us?

You see, when we take it personally, our eyes are focused downward -- onto ourselves. We're saying, "Look how this affects me!" -- "I am hurting over this!" The focus turns inward. When we turn inward, it starts to look pretty hopeless. Doesn't it?

Let's take a look at what God's Word tells us to do in Hebrews 12:2: "Let us fix our eyes on Jesus, the author and perfecter of our faith, who for the joy set before Him endured the cross, scorning its shame, and sat down at the right hand of the throne of God."

Jesus had some things happen that He could have taken very personally. He was facing pain we could not even fathom. He was facing the cross because of the actions of others. Yet, look at what He did. He knew the joy that would come in the end, so He endured the cross. He had His eyes on what the Father wanted. We need to keep our eyes on Jesus and follow the example He gave us in the midst of His trials.

Go on to verse 3: "Consider Him (Jesus) who endured such opposition from sinful men, so that you will not grow weary and lose heart." This is the reason we must look to Jesus -- so we do not grow weary and lose heart. Have you felt worn out and hopeless in some situations with the choices your children have made? Then it's time to stop taking it personally, and start personally taking it to Jesus.

Mama Bear to the Rescue

You've more than likely seen it in your neighborhood. It's the 'Mama bear' phenomenon. The kids are playing on the swing set in the backyard. Mary won't get off the swing to let someone else take a turn -- so your little Susie hits her. Mary runs home crying. Mary's Mom becomes much like a Mama bear. Her main mission in life is to protect her little 'cubbette'. She can't very easily separate herself from the hurt her little one has just experienced. She has a much more difficult time separating her feelings from the child who did the hurting -- your little Susie!

Once Mamma bear's child is hurt, she stands guard so it will never happen again. Her trust level for your Susie is greatly reduced. Susie is always the suspect when trouble arises in the neighborhood. If Mary comes running home crying, the first thing she thinks is your little Susie probably hit her again.

Haven't we done it ourselves? As Mothers, we are tied so closely on an emotional level it is very difficult to separate the child from what took place and begin to trust them again.

Forgiveness is the Key to Forgetting

So then, how do we separate the sin from the sinner -- especially in the middle of severe disappointment? We can't do it on our own. I've tried! We need to confess how we feel -- angry, sad, disappointed. Then, ask Jesus to help us to forgive. Forgiveness is the key. Then we need to ask Jesus to help us forget and never bring it up again.

Never bringing it up again was a tough one for me to overcome. I always seemed to remember past mistakes Matt had made. The key to never bringing it up again (forgetting) is to forgive. Only Jesus can teach us and enable us to forgive our children.

Whether it's a little hurt or disappointment or a huge sin that looms in your child's life -- the key to forgetting is forgiving. Let Jesus do that in and through you.

They Begin to Choose on Their Own

Isn't that what we want for our children? We want them to grow up to be independent adults -- capable of making their own decisions. We want them to leave the nest and be responsible adults. This process begins when they are young. We start by allowing them to make small choices. It might be which shirt they wear or which green vegetable we should make for dinner tonight. (In our house, it wasn't 'if' we should eat vegetables but 'which one' we should eat tonight.) We want them to begin to choose on their own while we are there to guide them. Then, decisions are slowly shifted over to them with less and less guidance as they grew and mature into adults.

We have tried to follow those guidelines with Matt. As he approached his older teens, we began to make the shift, encouraging him to make more decisions with our guidance. From the time Matt was young, he learned Philippians 4:6, "Don't worry about anything; instead pray

62

about everything..."(TLB). So, we stressed to him all decisions should be made by praying and asking God what He wanted him to do.

When he left home and was out on his own, he would have experience making his own choices. He would also have experienced the joys of taking everything to Jesus instead of just charging out there on his own.

Let's Put It to the Test

One Sunday evening, when Matt was 17, a friend from the youth group came by to see if he was going to attend the youth service that night. Matt said, "No, I'm too tired." I know he didn't pray. I know he didn't seek God's guidance as we had taught him to do. He just did what he wanted to do. I was angry at his self-centered behavior. I was sad because I felt we had raised him to know and love Jesus and now he was doing what he wanted to do -- not what God wanted him to do. I was sad because he was turning his back on what we had taught him. I wanted to jerk him off the couch and say, "You will go because I said so!"

Yet, weren't we trying to enable Matt to trust Jesus to help him make choices in his life? Yes, there would be times he would make those choices on his own without our help and without asking Jesus. That was his choice. We, of course, hoped he would pray about everything. At that time in Matt's life, it was to be left up to him. There would be some choices he would make with which we might not agree. This was one of the hardest parts of being a parent -- allowing him to begin to make choices.

Part of allowing him to grow up was letting him begin to make choices and then living with the disappointment when he didn't choose our way. You see our job as parents is to train them up in the ways of the Lord so that they know what God wants. This is why it is so important for us to point them to God's Word as the standard for their lives. This is why we cannot stand back and say, "Do whatever you want." We need to train them up as small children so when they become young adults, we no longer choose for them. We allow them to choose with the solid foundation of Jesus Christ under-girding them.

Why Train?

Train a child in the way he should go? Why bother? I've seen children turn out just fine, whose parents didn't do a thing to train them. On the other hand, I've seen parents who have diligently trained, only to watch their children throw it all away and chose an ungodly lifestyle. It caused those parents so much pain. I've seen the 'whys' in their eyes, too.

I asked that question myself when Matt was in his early twenties. We definitely didn't train him perfectly but we did try our best to point him to Jesus and the way he should go in his life. When he seemed to lay aside everything we had said was important, it felt as if all of our effort as parents had been in vain. Why did we spend so much energy and love in trying to bring him up to know Jesus, when eventually he would just lay it aside?

Then it hit me! John 14:15 says, "If you love Me, you will obey what I command." His command is to train up our children in the way they should go. We train our children because it is what Jesus asks us to do. We don't train them up so that they will do everything right or turn out perfect or make us proud.

Sometimes we tend to think that if we fill all the right squares, everything will turn out right. If we train them, our children will do everything they are supposed to do. Yes, training can produce results but that is not the reason we train. We train them up because of our love for Jesus and our desire to follow His commands. Obedience based on love.

How Old is Old?

Remember Proverbs 22:6? It says, "Train a child in the way he should go, and when he is old he will not turn from it." I love the second part of that verse that says, "and when he is old he will not turn from it." Notice it doesn't say, "when he is young he will not turn from it." It says "when he is old." This tells me there may a period of time when our children choose to turn away and do things their own way. Even with the best Christian upbringing, they may choose to go their own way. They may even turn their back on church or even on you for a while.

From personal experience, I can assure you -- **you will** survive the brokenness your heart feels while they are turning away. Remember -- it's our job to train them up to know Jesus and to follow His ways. They will then come to a point in their own lives where they will have to choose whom they will follow. They must choose between their own desires or the desires of their Lord.

Remember the promise at the end of this verse: "...when they are old they will not turn from it." Of course, it's always good to remember that only Jesus knows how old 'old' really is. For some of our children, 'old' may be when they are in college. For some children, 'old' may be when they're in their thirties or forties. Nevertheless, the promise Jesus gives in this Scripture is valid. You just do the job of training. Trust Jesus to do His work in their lives.

About a year ago, our son Matt packed up and moved to Buffalo, New York. We recently made a trip to see him, for the first time since his move. As we talked one morning, he said, "Mom and Dad, I may not go to church right now but I've never stopped praying. I talk to God everyday."

Of course, we want him back in church so he can receive the blessings of walking with Jesus and in being in fellowship with other Christians. I also believe what the Scripture says. Those things that we trained were laid aside but I see Matt gradually taking up some of those values and making them his own. I see a fine young man rising up.

Moms, you go right on training and teaching your children. Don't get discouraged when you don't see results. Trust Jesus to do the work in their lives.

If He Can Rebuild a Nation - He Can Rebuild Your Child

One morning, when Matt was in high school, I was going through a particularly fearful time. I knew there were some habits that had been formed in Matt's life that would eventually catch up with him. I feared the consequences. As I prayed about what to read in my Bible for my devotions, Jesus took me to the book of Jeremiah for what I felt was going to be a badly needed dose of encouragement.

As I read in chapter 4, all I saw throughout the chapter was God punishing Israel (His people) for turning away from Him. Verse 18 said, "Your own conduct and actions have brought this upon you. This is your punishment. How bitter it is! How it pierces to the heart!"

Now I even felt more discouraged about Matt because I felt like the Bible was saying, "If His sin (his conduct and actions) get too bad, I'll turn My back on Matthew, too." (Now remember Moms, we can't trust what we are feeling or thinking -- we need to ask Jesus, through the Holy Spirit, to explain the Word of God.)

When I prayed and asked Jesus to help me understand what this Scripture meant to me, here is what He spoke to my heart: "Just as with Israel, My people, -- Matt is one of My people. I must let My people go their own way and they may choose to follow the world. I will let Matt choose and follow whom he may but he still belongs to Me. It causes Me anguish when he turns away but you must trust that I will destroy the walls he has built around himself just as I destroyed the walls of the city surrounding Israel."

Verse 27 says, "...the whole land will be ruined, though I will not destroy it completely." In my heart, I heard Jesus say, "Yes, Matt may suffer the effects of his choices but he will not be destroyed completely. The land he now walks (not my path) will be ruined but I will preserve Matt."

Then I began to read in Jeremiah 30:18-b, "...the city will be rebuilt on her ruins, and the palace will stand in its proper place." That's it! Only once the corrupt nation is destroyed, can God begin to rebuild it into a mighty nation once again. He began to show me it was the same with Matthew. His little nation (the worldly paths he had chosen or the bad habits he had formed) will fall. It is all very necessary before he can be rebuilt into a mighty nation -- a mighty man of God. Then on top of the ruins will be built a palace. When God tears down -- He rebuilds something much better in its place.

Jeremiah 30:19 goes on to say, "From them will come songs of thanksgiving and the sound of rejoicing..." That's what needed to come from me. Songs of thanksgiving and sounds of rejoicing -- knowing that God will do the rebuilding.

Jesus ended with these words to me: "Don't fear for Matt -- only pray for him. Don't worry, Connie, If I can rebuild the nation of Israel -- I can rebuild your son."

What an encouragement those words were to me. When I saw Matt stuck in some of his old habits, I didn't need to

66

fear his destruction. I knew Matt trusted Jesus as his Savior, so I trust with my whole heart Jesus will never let him go. John 10:28-29 says, "I give them eternal life, and they shall never perish; no one can snatch them out of My hand. My Father, who has given them to Me, is greater than all; no one can snatch them out of My Father's hand." Moms, what a wonderful promise that is to us!

I also know Matt is allowed to make choices. Many of those choices will be right and some of them will be wrong. Our children are human so they will make mistakes. Jesus loves Matt enough to let him go -- knowing He alone has the power to set him free and rebuild him into a mighty man of God.

Jesus can rebuild my son even as He rebuilt the nation of Israel. He can do this for your child, too.

Don't Concentrate on Their Weaknesses

As Mothers, we know all of our child's weak spots. Some of us concentrate on them. (I was a concentrator!!) Some of us are blind to them. Neither is good. We need to ask Jesus how to view our children.

As Matt was getting ready to leave home after high school graduation, I knew he was a good student, didn't take drugs and wasn't out accumulating speeding tickets every weekend. I also knew his weak areas and tended to fear them and think about them more than his strengths. If you are a perfectionist, you'll be shaking your head about now because you understand this feeling first hand. It doesn't matter how many strengths a child has; a perfectionist will always see the weaknesses first.

Don't Miss the Real Lesson

When Matt was a junior in high school, one of his teachers required each student to enter the science fair as part of their class grade. Matt was a great student and extremely intelligent but not necessarily what you would term an overachiever. (This is not a bad thing -- unless the Mom happens to be an overachiever like me.) While Matt was satisfied to meet the minimum requirements of the project, I would have knocked myself out to excel and win first place. I was also feeling a little frustrated at the choice he made for his project. It was too simple -- too elementary for his intelligence level. I knew he was capable of far more than that. Although I didn't say anything to him, I was sure he sensed my disapproval and lack of excitement as he explained his project plans.

The day of the science fair arrived. Imagine my surprise when his simple, elementary project took first place in his category and he was advanced to the district science fair! Later when everything was over and the project came back home; I read the written report accompanying his project. This is what his dedication page said: "I would like to thank first of all, my parents for their support . . . and finally, I would like to thank the Lord for helping me through this time and for His support."

I wanted Matt to excel -- to be the best. Jesus was more interested in having Matt see His hand in completing the project. The dedication page contained the real lesson of the science fair project -- not the results of the project or awards he received.

If you have a tendency to concentrate on the weaknesses of your child -- you can join me now and ask Jesus to show you the entire lesson. I believe Jesus' goal is not to make us or our child perfect. (This will only come when we go to heaven to be with Him.) His goal is to take imperfect people and teach them to lean on Him in their weaknesses.

Today is the time to begin seeing Jesus working through your child's weaknesses. Don't miss the real lesson.

Remember to Encourage

If you struggle to see the strengths in your children, today you can ask Jesus to give you new eyes to see them. Most of the time, my fears only pointed out to Matt what I saw wrong. I was so fearful about what he was doing wrong I could never see him do anything right.

When he was about five years old and started talking to his friends on the phone, I stood right there listening and correcting his every word. I wanted him to talk on the phone properly. If he said someone at school was picking on him, I immediately quizzed him on what he did to cause it. I always assumed he was wrong. Talk about discouraging! Nothing he did was ever 'right' enough. No wonder he felt like giving up.

I am thankful that God kept some great positive Christians around me to remind me to encourage Matt more. Proverbs 15:1 also reminded me, "A gentle answer turns away wrath, but a harsh word stirs up anger". This is the way I can encourage -- with a gentle answer. I am also thankful the Word of God shows me a great reason to encourage. Hebrews 3:13 says, "But encourage one another daily, as long as it is called Today, so that none of you may be hardened by sin's deceitfulness." We are to encourage on a **daily** basis so the hearts of others aren't hardened and deceived. Criticism destroys confidence and hope. If someone is constantly criticized, it causes their heart to harden against the one who is criticizing them. Eventually it will harden their heart against God. Encouragement keeps the heart soft so sin can't take hold and deceive.

Do you want to keep the hearts of your children soft toward you and toward God? This is what encouragement does. For some of us -- it doesn't come very easily. We can ask Jesus to enable us to be encouragers -- through His strength. He will show us how.

Blindness Goes Both Ways

On the other hand, if you are a Mom who never sees the faults of your children -- you are just as blind as the Mom who sees every wrong. You also will need to ask Jesus to give you new eyes to see your children. It is just as destructive to blindly look at them -- refusing to see the areas where they need correction and guidance as it is to be blind to their strengths.

The Bible says in Romans 3:23, "for all have sinned and fall short of the glory of God." All means all -- even our children. With this fact in mind, remember that when children sin they need their parents to be there to correct them and cause them to come to repentance. We should never want to let our children get away with sin. Sin separates them from God. Our whole desire should be to bring them to repentance so they will ask Jesus for forgiveness and restore their relationship with God.

If we ignore their sin or even think their disobedience is 'kinda cute' -- we will eventually be hurting them. (Remember that something cute in a one year old becomes obnoxious and rebellious in a ten year old.) Don't be blind to the areas of weakness in your children. Jesus will let you see these areas so you can help your children turn to Him. When they turn to Him, He can change them.

Fear a Repeat Performance

Many times, we fear because of past mistakes our children have made. We're afraid they'll make the same mistake again and we'll see a repeat performance. We hover over them -- watching -- keeping guard as if we are capable of preventing any further mistakes in their lives.

If we look back in Genesis chapter 4, we see Eve with her two sons Cain and Abel. Imagine how she must have felt when Cain killed his brother Abel. He was then sent out to become a wanderer forever. Eve not only had to endure the pain of losing one son to death but she also knew she may never see her other son again because of the consequences of his sin. As mothers, we feel the pain of our children. We also feel the pain our children cause others.

Amidst her pain, Eve may have experienced the fear Cain would go out and hurt once again. He had done it once. Was he capable of doing it again? Eve was no more able to prevent repeat mistakes for Cain than we are for our children.

So Moms, what do we do with the fear? Remember this: Jesus loves your children much more than you are ever capable of loving them. And because He loves with a perfect love, we know the words of I John 4:18-19 are true. The Living Bible says, "We need have no fear of someone who loves us perfectly; His perfect love for us eliminates all dread of what He might do to us. If we are afraid, it is for fear of what He might do to us, and shows that we are not fully convinced that He really loves us. So you see, our love for Him comes as a result of His loving us first." Jesus loves our children with a perfect love. This perfect love eliminates all the dread of what He might do to us or to our children. Leave the fear and worry about repeat performances to Him.

It's Dangerous to Compare

Matt was off to college and I had been fervently praying for over a year that Jesus would send him a Christian friend. I felt a Christian friend would help, encourage and strengthen him. I just knew this was what Matt needed.

70

Then I talked to a friend who had just sent her son off to college. This young man was a strong Christian with a faith that never seemed to waiver. When he got to college, his room mate turned out to be a strong Christian. "Hey -- wait a minute! I have been praying Matt would get a Christian friend. Her son is already strong enough in his faith and he gets the Christian roommate! Matt didn't! It's not fair, Lord! Don't you remember my prayers? Don't you love them the same? Why can't you do the same thing for Matt?"

"By the way, why can't Matt be just like her son?" Oh -- Moms. It's dangerous to compare.

Christianity is Not a Group Event

God created Matt as an individual, not as a group. There is no one in the world exactly like our Matt. God sent His Son, Jesus, to die for Matt as an individual. Matt's relationship with Jesus is personal -- not a group event.

I have come to understand that just as Matt was created as an individual and received salvation as an individual, Jesus will treat him as an individual. He will never treat Matt exactly the same as He treats someone else. This is the beauty and wonder of having a living, personal relationship with Jesus Christ.

Mom, if you compare your children to other children -- you will be setting yourself up for frequent disappointment. If you remember Jesus knows your children personally and will do the best for them -- you will never be disappointed. It's dangerous to compare!

Jesus loves our children much more than we would ever be capable of loving them. As Moms, we think we know what they need. As their Savior, He knows exactly what they need -- and it's not always exactly what someone else's child needs.

If Jesus gave Matt everything I thought he needed, it could be all the wrong things. If I had my way, it might short circuit a lesson He was trying to teach Matt or might prevent his faith from being strengthened through a difficult situation.

The one thing you need to remember -- You are only their Mom. He is their God!

71

Down in the Dumps - Deeper Than Dirt -
With No Hope Left in My Heart

Have you been down in the dumps, that low -- deeper than dirt? Have you felt there was no hope left in your heart? This can happen when children disappoint us so deeply that we feel as if all hope is lost. All those hopes and dreams brought into our lives by that little baby, are now shattered and torn.

When Matt graduated from high school and decided not to go to college right away, I was crushed. From the time he was born, I had hoped, planned and prepared for the day he would leave for college. I would pack everything he needed for dorm life. I would send him survival packages of cookies. He would drive home from college for holidays and eagerly tell us about all of his classes. When that didn't happen and Matt chose to serve some military duty, I was down in the dumps. I could feel myself sliding 'deeper than dirt' and each day my hope that he would graduate from college began to get dimmer and dimmer.

Now to some of you Moms, this may sound petty. So what? He didn't follow my college plans. He stepped out and made plans of his own. This is what young people are supposed to do. Yet, I still felt the bottom drop out of my hopes and dreams.

I know some of you have experienced far greater disappointments than changed college plans. Some of you may have children who have broken the law or are even in prison. The crime may be so unspeakable that friends and family act as if your child was never born. It has not only brought you shame and disgrace but there is no hope left in your heart.

Others may have children headed down the wrong path, who refuse to change directions. They may have already suffered some of the consequences and still refuse to turn back. Some have even run away from home. You have no hope left in your heart.

You see warning signs in your very young children. You watch them play and interact with friends and you see danger ahead. What will happen when they grow up? What if...? Soon, you have no hope left in your heart.

Don't Go on Results

We live in a very 'result oriented' society, don't we? If they produce the best -- we're ecstatic. If they produce less than the best -- we're disappointed.

Is God 'result oriented'? We can see from the Scriptures that certain actions carry consequences -- results. This is a fact of life. However, we also see that God's Word holds very few references to results but over five hundred references to the heart. God is always looking beyond results to the heart. He wants to reach the hearts of your children.

Yes, it is a fact that your children and mine will suffer the consequences of their actions. We all have wilderness experiences. So must our children. It is in the wilderness that their hearts will be tested. God is 'heart oriented'. He wants to change our children from the inside-out. No. He doesn't go on results. He concentrates on the place where it all begins -- the heart.

Our Hope is in Jesus

While they are being tested, you may not feel you have any hope left. I understand this feeling. It is a powerless feeling, difficult for a Mom to experience. After all, she is the one who fixed everything when it was broken. When it all began, she fed and rocked to quiet the tears. A few years ago, Band-Aids and kisses fixed any boo-boo. Just yesterday, hugs and soothing words repaired the deepest disappointments. Today, there may be nothing a Mom can do to fix her child or make the hurt go away.

There is only One who can. His name is Jesus. He is our Hope. You may have come to the end of your rope and feel there is no hope left. I realize it may not feel like it but you are actually in a good spot because you know you are helpless. Once you know you can't fix it, you have come to the point at which you can turn to Jesus and let Him be the hope for your child. (In other words, we finally realize we need to step out of the way and let Jesus be their hope.)

Psalm 31:24 says, "Be strong and take heart, all you who hope in the Lord." When you are 'down in the dumps -- deeper than dirt', you can take heart if your hope is in the Lord. Isn't this great news! We don't have to be strong in our own strength. We can be strong because our hope is in Jesus.

There will be times in our lives, when our children disappoint us. Some of those may be small disappointments and others may be so overwhelming that we feel our hope is destroyed. I can tell you this: there is One who will never disappoint you. In Isaiah 49, we read from the last part of verse 23: "...Then you will know that I am the Lord; those who hope in Me will not be disappointed." Put your hope in Jesus. You will never be disappointed!

The Blame Game

Psychologists, counselors, and well meaning authors say -- "if only the parents had raised them right, this wouldn't have happened. They are a victim of their upbringing." You can bring up your children in the church. You can teach them about Jesus. As a Christian mother, you can do everything you possibly can to raise your children right. These children can still choose to follow a different path. It's called free will. God gave us all a free will. He gave us guidelines. He even planted knowledge of right and wrong in our hearts. He also allowed us the freedom to choose which path we would take. It's time to stop the blame game.

The Word is 'Choose'

I believe it is very important to understand that the word is 'choose'. Our children make choices -- they choose. No one, even their parents, force them to make wrong choices. There is no one to blame when they choose the wrong path. The responsibility is theirs.

When they are young, our job is to help form and direct them so when they are older, they will have learned which is the right path. This is why we are to discipline our children. Discipline teaches them that wrong choices have consequences. When your children are still young, remember this point: Discipline is not a hateful thing. It is a loving action toward our children. Our hearts should say, "I love my children and want the best for them. This is why I am disciplining them -- so they learn which path is the right path and not have to suffer the pain of wrong choices later in life."

There are times when they will choose the right path and others when they will choose what is wrong. It will be their choice.

When we are training our children, it is good to make sure they understand that they are responsible for their own choices. Teach them to never play the 'blame game'. Teach them that they choose and the best way to make the right choices in their life is to follow Jesus.

Don't Pack Those Bags So Fast!

Now in case you are packing your bags for a guilt trip -- I'd like to share something with you. I've been on that trip and the ticket says 'one way'. You see, when Matt was young, I frequently disciplined out of frustration or anger. I had a terrible habit of waiting and waiting until I couldn't stand it any longer and then I would explode. I know now I should have disciplined him immediately, before I got to the explosive stage. I realize discipline should always be out of love, not frustration or anger. I know I didn't do all I should have in training Matt when he was young. I should have done so much more to help direct him towards the right path. Many times I let disobedience slide because I was tired. I should have been more consistent with discipline. I should have used God's Word as my guideline. Even from the time he was a toddler, I could have shown him in the Bible why a particular action was wrong. Even though I knew those were the right ways to train up a child, I just didn't do all those right things.

I do know one thing: I did the very best I could at the time. Yes, as I look back now, I see all I could have done. I'm much older and much wiser than I was twenty three years ago.

Looking back at the 'why didn't I's' cannot change the past. The only reason to look back is to ask Jesus for forgiveness in the areas where I failed.

Look Towards Today

We all have times in our lives when we aren't doing all we should be. I realize now, that I did the very best I could have at the time. I believe you will also find this true in your life. We did the very best we could with the knowledge and ability we possessed at that time in our lives.

So, unpack those bags headed for a guilt trip. Don't look back. Only look forward to all Jesus wants you to be for your child now -- today. It's not too late.

Keep on Praying

There were times when I was so disappointed, angry, frustrated or disheartened, I felt like giving up. It was during one of those times Jesus reminded me I should never give up praying for Matt.

Prayer is one of the greatest and most loving tools Jesus has given us as mothers. Ephesians 6:18 (TLB) says, "Pray all the time. Ask God for anything in line with the Holy Spirit's wishes. Plead with Him, reminding Him of your needs, and keep on praying earnestly for all Christians everywhere." Are you praying all the time for your children? Are you pleading with God; reminding Him of your needs?

Keep on praying for your children. Never give up on them -- but be sure to give them up to Jesus.

You'll Never Be Disappointed

Life is full of disappointments but the Scripture tells us we never have to be disappointed again. Romans 10:11 (TLB) says, "For the Scriptures tell us that no one who believes in Christ will ever be disappointed."

This doesn't mean there aren't things in our lives that let us down. It is saying, when those times arrive, we will never be disappointed if we believe in Christ. He will carry us through the hard times. He will give us strength. He will be all our children need. He will be all that we need.

Let me tell you what happened when Matt was a sophomore in college and coming home for Christmas break. I was excited about having him home, yet apprehensive about the whole situation. You see, Matt had a job earlier in the school year but quit when his knees starting causing him problems. That meant he was coming home for Christmas with no job and no money -- and for him, no real anxiety about the situation.

Truthfully, getting a present for Christmas was not the issue. What was important to me was the fact he didn't think enough about others to show he cared about them. I thought we had taught him better.

The closer it got to Christmas, the more anxious I got. Then I got angry when we talked over the phone. He seemed so laid back about Christmas and his lack of funds.

In my head, I could imagine what was about to happen. He'd come home from college and announce he didn't have any money so he would have to buy presents after Christmas. The more I thought about it the angrier I got. I was so disappointed he wasn't thinking about others.

Jesus and I had a few long discussions about this situation (with me doing most of the talking). When I finally stopped to listen, I remembered the words, "..no one who believes in Christ will ever be disappointed." If those words were true -- I needed to start acting as if they were true. That's the point at which the attitude of my heart began to change. No matter what happened this Christmas, I didn't have to be disappointed because I had Christ. He would be all that I needed even when my child might disappoint me.

(To end the story: Two days before Christmas Matt arrived home. He nonchalantly announced he sold a couple old textbooks and was going out to buy presents. Now I'll have to admit, his method and timing were rather unorthodox. Different than mine but none the less effective. He's a great young man, with a free spirit. He keeps life exciting for this structured, not-always-flexible Mom!)

The point of this whole story is to share with you how easily we seem to let disappointments overtake us. I'm not immune to disappointments. None of us are. Matt could have come home that Christmas with no money for presents and no solution in sight.

Yes, our children may disappoint us but those who believe in Christ will never be disappointed. Let Jesus be your hope today.

Our prayer can be:

Father, You know how much I love these children You have given me. They have brought such joy and love into my life. Please remind me, Lord, when I tend to be disappointed by their actions, that they are human and will make mistakes. Help me to love them through those times. Help me to remember that You are my hope and their hope, too. When they look into the eyes of their Mother, help them to see the hope of Jesus shining bright.

When I feel inadequate, help me to remember that all I'm not -- You are. Father, I trust You to be their God and I promise to just be their Mom.

In Jesus' name I pray.
Amen.

How would you answer these questions?:

1. Would you classify yourself as a guiding or controlling Mom?

2. What can you do to help your children take responsibility for their own actions?

3. Read Proverbs 22:6. Write down in your own words what it means to you and your children.

4. Are you feeling hopeless? Today, find someone who will pray with you and for you.

5

I Want to be the Best Mom in the World - So Then Why Do I Feel Like the Worst ??...

Because I've Made So Many Mistakes !!

Well, join the club! We have all made mistakes -- and plenty of them.

Through a very thorough search, I've found there is no space on a birth certificate next to the names of the parents where it says 'prone to errors'. There should be! They should warn children from the time they are born that parents aren't perfect. We all know it's true.

We see our mistakes with close up vision. You can't miss them. They are a glaring reality. We have to face them every day. I know I did!

Training Didn't Help

By profession, I was a registered nurse. With that kind of training, you would think being a Mom should be a snap! I was trained to take care of sick people, pregnant women, heart attack victims and more. I even did some training in pediatrics. Just throw a challenge at me and I was ready to conquer!

When Matt was about two months old, he began crying for hours on end. I did the normal, change the wet diaper routine. I tried to feed him. I bounced and burped him. He still cried. It didn't matter if it was day or night; he just kept on crying. He had no fever. He wasn't drawing up his legs in pain. He wasn't rubbing his ears or eyes. He just cried for hours until I finally cried along with him.

This went on for about a week. Finally, out of sheer desperation, I took him into the doctor. I found out he had severe ear infections in both ears. How could I have missed it? I was a nurse. I'm supposed to know those kinds of things. I was trained. I let my little baby suffer with pain for a week before I took him to the doctor.

What kind of Mom was I? How could I make a dumb mistake like that!!

I Was a Repeat Offender

You say, "Everyone makes mistakes." You're right -- but I kept making them. Matt was about two years old and was attending a day care program while I worked. One summer evening when I was giving him his bath, I noticed little raised bumps all over his chest and back. Now to me, they looked like bites from red sand ants so prevalent in the area of Florida where we lived. "I can't believe those stupid teachers would let the kids out into the sandbox where there are thousands of ants. Look at him! He's covered with bites! I'm going to school tomorrow and give them a piece of my mind!"

I got Matt up the next morning to get him dressed and my heart sank as deep as my toes. Now I could tell those bumps weren't ant bites. All those spots were chicken pox! How could I make a mistake like that! I was a nurse! Wouldn't I ever learn? I was a repeat offender. It seemed as if I was making the same mistakes over and over again.

The Easy Road Was Lined With Rocks

When Matt was just a toddler, I knew he should drink water or fruit juice in his cup but many times I filled it with Kool-aid. I knew it was a bad choice. I knew it and still did it because it was easier. I was disciplined in so many areas, except when it came to my child. Many times I did the easiest thing instead of the right thing. Oh, the easy road was lined with rocks. I kept stumbling over them as I made one mistake after another. What was wrong with me? Other Moms didn't make mistakes like this -- did they?

When he was a toddler, my days were filled with my job, household duties, church work. To keep him occupied, so I could get everything done, I let him watch TV. Although I knew too much TV was bad for him; I let TV become his baby-sitter. In the preteen years, he watched too much violence. I knew I should stop it but didn't.

As a note, I want to mention something for those of us who are married. Don't think I'm saying I was totally responsible for Matt watching too much TV. Dad should have a hand in those limits, as well. I am saying the times when I was alone with Matt, I should have limited what he watched. When we were together as a family, I could have expressed my concern about TV to my husband. We could have worked together to set and enforce limits.

The years went by and soon it was too late. Our son was out on his own, making his own choices. In some of those areas where I was undisciplined, I could now see Matt was undisciplined. Why didn't I work on this when he was younger? Why didn't I make him do this when I could? Why did I pick the easy road?

Don't Get Stuck on Regret Circle

"Why didn't I? Why did I?" These are questions every Mother seems to ask. When we ask them and set right out to answer them ourselves, you know what the answer will be. "I told you that you were a terrible Mom. You did it again! You blew it!"

Those 'why' questions are all right to ask if you let Jesus answer them for you. He never sets out to accuse. He will always give you wisdom and guidance. It says in Romans 11:33 (TLB), "Oh, what a wonderful God we have! How great are His wisdom and knowledge and riches! How impossible it is for us to understand His decisions and His methods!" Isn't that true? We think we deserve to hear Him say, "You blew it again! How could you!" Yet, we hear Him say, "Yes, it was a mistake. I love you and I'll give you wisdom and knowledge to help you not make the same mistake again."

What gets us into trouble is repeatedly asking these same questions. Why -- Why -- Why? We ask them and we don't really want His answer because we already have the condemning answer in our heads. We're merely regretting our actions. Most of the time, it gets us stuck on Regret Circle. This is when all we can see is our mistakes. We have our eyes down so low we can't see a way out of the circle and so we keep going round and round. There is no end to Regret Circle. It keeps covering the same ground, over and over again.

8 1

I've made a few trips around Regret Circle in my lifetime. I almost got stuck there again last summer. Mike and I were watching an old video of Matt taken when he was about six years old. As I watched, my heart sank as I realized I constantly criticized and corrected Matt. Oh, it wasn't out-right nagging. I was more subtle than that. It just seemed that by my reactions caught on videotape, he could never do anything right. I always had a better way for him to do it. I cringed as I saw myself in action and promised myself I wouldn't fall into that trap again. This time, I was committed to stopping myself before it started.

Several hours later, Matt came home from his summer job. He had a rough evening at work with one of the supervisors. He no more than got those words out of his mouth, when I caught myself correcting him and telling him a better way he could have handled things at work. Oh no! I did it again! I promised I wouldn't and it didn't take more than five minutes in the room with him before I broke the promise. I was at it again!

As I felt the disappointment and discouragement in myself, my eyes went down and stayed on me. "What's wrong with me? Will I ever change? Why do I keep doing the same thing over and over again?" I could feel myself getting stuck on Regret Circle. Then I remembered what it said in Hebrews 12:2 (TLB): "Keep your eyes on Jesus, our leader and instructor. He was willing to die a shameful death on the cross because of the joy He knew would be His afterwards; and now He sits in the place of honor by the throne of God." Jesus saw many people make mistakes as they mocked Him, beat Him and nailed Him to the cross. He was willing to forgive their mistakes because He knew the final outcome. He is willing to forgive our mistakes, too.

Do you get tired of battling the same mistakes? I did that night Matt came home from work. Listen to the rest of Hebrews 12:3-4 (TLB): "If you want to keep from becoming faint hearted and weary, think about His patience as sinful men did such terrible things to Him. After all, you have never yet struggled against sin and temptation until you sweat great drops of blood." That's true. I have struggled with the same mistake but never until I sweat drops of blood. I'm not ready to give up because Jesus hasn't given up on me!

I had a choice that night. I could keep looking down and only see my mistakes or I could look up and see Jesus. Jesus knows my mistakes and yet, in spite of this, He hasn't given up on me. When I'm honest with Him about my mistakes, He is always ready to forgive me and show me the way He wants me to live. Don't get stuck on Regret Circle. It's a dead-end street. Lift your eyes up to Jesus. He'll never give up on you!

Groups of Mistakes

When Matt was two years old, we moved from Colorado to Florida. We were temporarily living in a small mobile home close to the Air Force base where Mike was stationed. We had only been there a couple of days when I packed up Matt and our basket of dirty laundry. We drove a couple hundred yards to the little laundromat located in the mobile home park. Matt's car seat was still in our other vehicle but my car was very small so I was sure I could keep my arm over his body as I drove. He stood close beside me so I knew he'd be safe for such a short distance. We threw the laundry in the machine and I decided to kill some time by driving down to a nearby shopping center. It was only about three blocks away. The car seat wouldn't make much difference for only three blocks. Besides, it was a extremely small compact car which meant Matt couldn't get far from my reach.

Matt stood next to me on the seat, as I turned left across the two oncoming lanes of traffic. I slowly and cautiously made the turn into the parking lot. All of a sudden, I heard the door open and I saw Matt in my rear view mirror. I had only taken my arm away from in front of him for a couple of seconds while I made the turn. He fell out of the car and was getting up off the pavement and running after the car. I must not have closed the car door hard enough. As I made the turn, he fell out of the car, right in the middle of a four lane road.

Now, I'd like to tell you I did what most normal mothers with a brain in their head would do. I'd like to tell you I immediately stopped the car in the middle of the oncoming lanes and picked up my child to keep him from any further danger. I can't tell you that because I didn't do it. Once I saw he was alive and running after the car, I kept slowly driving the car another twenty to thirty feet. For some reason, I was concerned about pulling my car into the safety of the shopping center driveway. I wish I could tell you why I did that. Why was I more concerned about my car getting hit than I was about my child getting hit? My choice wasn't rational. It wasn't logical. It wasn't even normal. What was wrong with me!

The first mistake I made was not putting him in the car seat. In his entire life, I never drove the car unless he was in his car seat. Yet, that day I left him out of the car seat. Mistake number two -- impulsively, I decided to drive down to the shopping center because I didn't want to be bored sitting around waiting for my laundry to get done. Mistake number three -- I didn't shut Matt's door tightly when I removed the laundry basket from the car. Mistake number four -- I didn't stop the car and immediately rescue my child once he fell out of the door. There were so many 'should haves' about the whole incident. How could I make so many mistakes all at one time? It wasn't enough I was a single mistake maker. I made most of my mistakes in big groups!

The Unforgivable Mistake

When I finally ran back and scooped Matt up into my arms, I could see the huge goose egg forming in the middle of his forehead. He said, "Mommy. Mommy. You dropped me out of the car on my head!" My mistakes cost my child physical and emotional pain. I felt so guilty. I could hardly face the fact I was an incompetent mother. It wasn't just letting him fall out of the car. It was also the fact I didn't respond immediately to his injury. Night after night for the next few weeks, I would have nightmares. I would hear the thump of another car hitting Matt. It was because I left him lying in the middle of the road instead of picking him up as any other normal mother would have done. In my eyes, I had committed the unforgivable mistake!

It took several years before Jesus helped me face that day and accept his forgiveness for the mistakes I made. He helped me to see even though I had made several mistakes that day, I had not intentionally hurt my child. My intention was not to throw him on the ground to hurt him. My goal for the day was not to injure Matt. In my heart, the thing I wanted to do more than anything was to love him.

We all make mistakes. No mistake is unforgivable if we only come to Jesus.

It's My Fault

Every time Matt made a wrong choice -- I felt responsible. I felt as if I had made a mistake causing him to do what he did. I'm not responsible. He is. Yes, I have had a great influence on his life but I do not cause Him to make wrong choices. My job is to point him the right way -- towards the right choices. Then, he is responsible for the choices he makes.

Too many times, in society today, children blame their parents for their choices. "It's because my parents abused me -- that's why I am a criminal." "I was poor as a child -- that's why I steal as an adult." Now, I understand some children grow up under extremely difficult circumstances -- alcoholic parents, abuse, poverty. These are terrible things but none of these conditions offer an excuse for continuing to make wrong choices in their lives.

The same is true for your children. No matter how many mistakes you have made as a mother, this does not offer your children an excuse for choosing to sin. Moms, please don't take the rap for your children. Yes, we need to accept the responsibility for our actions -- for our mistakes. We need to ask our children for forgiveness when we are wrong. However, we can't let them blame us for the way they are today. Blaming us only lets them escape from facing the truth. The truth is Jesus can heal any past wound. Jesus can forgive any mistake a parent makes. Our children must face the truth and when they do, they will discover the freedom that blaming others would never offer them.

Our son, Matt, drove this point home recently. I was having an extreme bout of the 'guilts' about some things I didn't do when he was a teen. He said, "Mom, it wouldn't have mattered what you did or said. I did what I did because I wanted to do it." Now that's maturity. He assumed responsibility for his actions and didn't place the blame on anyone else.

We also must quit accepting blame. If we have gone to Jesus to ask for His forgiveness for our mistakes, it is time to let go of the blame. If we always claim responsibility, our children will never have to accept responsibility for their own actions. Help your children grow by not taking the blame when it does not belong to you.

Big or Small - They Feel the Same

Some of us have made a few big, huge mistakes. Some of us have made many little, tiny mistakes. Big or small -- mistakes all feel the same, don't they? Those little mistakes can add up until they begin to feel like a knot that sits in the pit of our stomachs. It then feels just the same as one of those monstrous mistakes. I had lots of both in my life -- many little, tiny mistakes and a few big, huge ones thrown in for good measure.

Am I the Only One Who Feels This Way?

I felt like such a failure. When Matt was little, I saw other Moms with their young children. I was sure they didn't feel the same way as I did. They looked confident and self assured.

Every brand new Mom I observed, seemed to just naturally know what to do for the little one in her arms. I didn't just naturally know what to do. Everyone said you could tell the difference between a 'hungry' cry and a 'wet' cry. Funny thing! I never could. I just learned that you check everything and eventually one of those things will fix the cry. No one else seemed to talked about their mistakes, so I assumed there weren't any.

I was sure I was the only one in the world who struggled with these feelings. I was the only one in the world who made so many mistakes.

We're All in the Same Boat

Oh, aren't we adept at hiding the real 'me'? Why is it so hard to admit we have made mistakes, especially in church or around our Christian friends?

Some years ago, I started attending a women's Bible study group. As we studied the lesson, women began to share some of their struggles with their children, husbands, friends. Wait a minute! Wait a minute! These women were real! They struggled with being a good Mom -- being a Godly wife -- living a Christ-like life. I found we were all in the same boat! We were all less than perfect. We had all made mistakes.

We All Have the Same Answer

What is more important, I found we all had the same answer. His name was Jesus. Jesus was bigger than any mistakes I had ever made. Jesus could forgive any mistake. Big or small -- no mistake was too tough for Him. As we shared our mistakes with each other, we also shared in the victory Jesus brought us through those mistakes. We don't just go around making mistakes so He can straighten them out. Yes, our mistakes do cost a price. The real hope is knowing when we do make mistakes, He is there to take us through them. He is there to forgive. He is there to teach and train. Jesus is always there.

Too Many Mistakes?

If you're saying, "You don't know me. I've made so many mistakes!" Remember there is a difference between <u>so many</u> mistakes and <u>too many</u> mistakes.

If you think you've made <u>so many</u> mistakes; you are in a great position. Then you realize how much you need Jesus. If you thought you were perfect and made no mistakes -- I would say you were in trouble. You probably wouldn't see your need for Jesus.

Do you think you have reached the 'mistake limit'? Remember Jesus never says, "Well, you've made <u>too many</u> mistakes. You've used up your quota. You're outta here! No more chances for you!"

We will all make mistakes. Have you accepted the forgiveness Jesus offers? He already paid the price for your mistakes. I John 1:9 says, "If we confess our sins, He is faithful and just and will forgive us our sins and purify us from all unrighteousness." He <u>will</u> forgive. It is a promise. Some of you might be saying, "You don't know what I've done. I can never forgive myself." If you have come to Jesus and confessed, the Scripture says He is faithful and just to forgive your sins.

I can't find anywhere in the Scripture where it says I have to forgive myself in order to make forgiveness real or valid. When I say, "I can't forgive myself", I am really saying I don't believe what Jesus did on the cross was good enough for me. I need to do something more.

That's a lie. Nothing more is needed. Jesus already did it all on the cross. You only need to receive it. It has already been done. Are you willing to accept His payment as sufficient for your mistakes? This is real forgiveness and it will set you free.

A Heart Check

What's in your heart? Is it to keep on making the same mistakes or to let Jesus change you? He looks at your heart. If you truly want Him to change you, ask Him today.

Do you know Jesus is the answer to the mistakes you have made as a Mom? Take them to Him. He'll forgive you. Let Him take the burden of guilt from your shoulders.

Pray with me:

Dear Father, I've made so many mistakes. You gave me these children and trusted me to care for them. So many times I've blown it. I've messed up. Please forgive.

You've seen every one of my mistakes and still You love me. Thank You for never giving up on me. Help me to accept Your forgiveness and move on from my mistakes.

In Jesus' name I pray,
Amen

T hink about these things:

1. Do I ever get stuck on Regret Circle? What regrets seem to take me there?

2. Are there any mistakes I've made that always come back to haunt me? Am I willing to take them to Jesus today?

6

I Want to be the Best Mom in the World -
So Then Why Do I Feel Like the Worst ??...

Because I'm Not Sure They Really Love Me !!

We all want to be loved, don't we? There is something about being loved that builds us up. Being loved can carry us through difficult times. Love gives us a sense of security and belonging. Maybe that's why some of us had children -- to be loved.

That Baby Kind of Love

Infants are entirely unconditional in their love. They want someone to hold them. They need to be fed. They love to have dry diapers. It doesn't take them long to bond with those who hold, feed and change them.

The memory of Matt as a baby is still clearly written on my mind. First thing each morning, he would gurgle and coo when he saw me walk into the room. It didn't matter if I had snapped at him the night before when he woke me up for the fourteenth time. It didn't make any difference if I had complained about his smelly diaper a few hours earlier. He saw me and his face lit up. Now, that's the baby kind of love -- unconditional. We've all felt it but...have there been times when you weren't sure if your children really loved you?

If They Loved Me...They'd Act Like It

I hate to admit it. I'm a results oriented individual. I want to see results, and of course, I want to see them directly related to my actions. So...if my child loved me...he'd act like it! As the old saying goes, "That ain't necessarily so!"

The Personality Factor

There are more factors in the 'love equation' to consider. One very important consideration is personality. It's just a fact of life that children are not born as a blank piece of paper, just waiting for you to write everything down you would like them to be. They are each born with a personality that has a great influence on their actions. You can observe this in some infants who are just born snugglers. When held, they wiggle until they're safely wedged between Mom's body and arms. Matt was definitely one of those babies. He was always happy to have me pick him up, smother him with kisses and hugs and hold him snugly against me.

At three years old, he loved to have me lie on the floor so he could sprawl right on top of me to watch his favorite TV show. When he was about five years old, he still thrived on that physical contact. He always wanted to hold my hand when we went walking or out shopping. Even now as a young adult, he feels free to hug Dad and Mom -- even in front of his friends or in public.

Not every child welcomes this close contact. Some infants just don't like to be held. It's not that someone had to teach them; they just naturally don't want to be too close or confined in someone's arms. If you had a baby who pulled away from physical contact, you may have felt he didn't love you. There is nothing wrong with you. It may just be part of the way the child is made. It has a lot to do with personality -- or as I like to say, "the way they're wired".

Some three year olds have an independence-bent personality and want to do everything by themselves. By five, some children would never think of holding their mother's hand in public. Children are all different. If you have more than one child in your family, you probably see the dynamics of all those individual personalities in action right under your own roof. Some of a child's outward expression of love is determined by their personality.

Environment Comes Into Play

A child's environment adds yet another dimension to how they express their love. When I was growing up, we were not a family of huggers. I knew, without a doubt, my Mom and Dad loved me but we weren't an overly expressive family with our love. We didn't go around hugging and kissing each other all the time. There was an understanding of the love we had for each other but not much outward display.

One of the most favorite times I remember with my Dad was driving to the dump. It doesn't sound like a very exciting event but the day it was my special turn is still burned in my memory. Before we drove off, he sat me on his lap and I got to hold the steering wheel and pretend to drive. In a couple of minutes, he placed me over on the seat beside him and off we drove. As we got older, Dad would give each one of us four girls a turn traveling on a day trip with him in his job as a salesman. What a treat -- eating in a restaurant, listening to my Dad hum to the tune of the radio and getting to have him all to myself. Those times said more to me about my Dad's love for me than words could ever express. It was his way of showing love.

As a child, I learned from my environment, as did my parents before me. Your children will, too. If they grow up with frequent physical expressions of love, they will probably express themselves on a physical level more easily. If they are a part of a less expressive family, chances are they also will react in much the same way.

As an adult, even though it was a little awkward at first, I began to hug my parents and tell them I loved them. Through this, we began to establish a more physical expression of our love. So, you see, it's never too late to begin hugging and holding your children today as you help form their habits for tomorrow.

Remember there are many ways to express love -- not just physical contact. Teaching our children to respect others and to speak kindly, also teaches them how to express love. I Corinthians 16:14 says, "Do everything in love." Make your home an environment where love is displayed in everything you do.

It's No Guarantee

It's true. There's no guaranteed outcome -- even if you have children with the demonstrative type of personality and have built an environment of open expression of love. You can do everything 'right'. There is still no guarantee that if your children love you; they'll act like it.

It's because our children are humans, with no guarantees on how they'll act at a given moment. We train them to 'act right' (like in front of our church friends) -- then they decide to do just the opposite. If they loved me -- they'd act like it! No guarantees. But why?

One Little Detail

There's one tiny detail called sin we must consider. How many of you have had to teach your sweet little toddler how to disobey? No? Did you have to teach them how to say "No" or "Mine"? No - They just naturally know how to do it -- even early on in life. Don't they? That's called original sin and we're all born with it. (Romans 3:23, "For all have sinned and fall short of the glory of God.")

As parents, we spend their entire childhood trying to teach them to obey. When we do this, we're teaching them to fight against their sinful nature that naturally loves to sin.

Our children are no different than adults. They are also given a free will. They can choose to obey or disobey -- just as we can. This is why, even if you do everything right -- there is still no guarantee they will <u>act</u> like they love you.

The Only Guarantee

The only guarantee you and I have as parents is the knowledge that we will always do our best to teach our children to obey God and to hate sin. We should want them to do this because of their love for Jesus. The way we can help them learn this is through discipline -- correcting them when they do something wrong.

Some parents don't want to discipline their children because they are afraid of making the children mad. And, yes -- discipline may make them mad. But listen to what it says in Proverbs 13:24 (TLB): "If you refuse to discipline your son, it proves you don't love him; for if you love him you will be prompt to punish him."

As Christian parents, we want our children to know that even when they don't act like they love us; we are always going to love them enough to discipline them. We do this so they will turn away from sin and turn toward Jesus.

If They Loved Me...They'd Say It

Isn't that how it's supposed to go? If they loved me...they'd say it. What's so hard about saying, "Mom, I love you!"? It's just four little words! Now, most toddlers are good at this one. Sometimes Matt would stop playing to come over and sit on my lap. He'd use his pudgy little hands to mash my cheeks together and give me a big, wet kiss as he said, "Mommy, I wuv you!" Those toddlers know how to get the message across.

No Longer #1

Then in grade school, his sphere of influence began to widen. Teachers and friends crowded me out and I was no longer the central figure in his life. I lost first place. Those verbal expressions of love I was used to receiving were no longer lavished on me quite as frequently. I didn't realize this can be a normal part of the process as children are seeking to establish independence. Sometimes I felt little twinges in my heart saying, "Maybe he really doesn't love me anymore."

You're a Mean Mom!

At about six years old, Matt wanted to have everything everyone else had and wanted to do everything else his friends were doing. "I'm sorry," I told him, "you're not everybody else." That was about as popular as rain at a picnic. At that point in his life, he not only wouldn't say, "Mom, I love you"; he said, "I don't even like you. You're a mean Mom!"

I was devastated! How could he say that? I was just trying to be a good Mom. I was so tempted to fold under the pressure and let him do whatever he wanted and have what everyone else had. I was almost willing to do anything so he would still love me. I couldn't risk losing his love -- could I?.

Don't Yield to the Pressure

Have you been there? Have your children gone even so far as to say, "I hate you!"? It hurts when our children react with words that wound. I want to encourage you not to yield to the pressure because you're afraid of losing their love.

Sometimes Matt reacted in anger when we had to say "no", especially in those pre-teen and teen years. He was hoping his angry reaction would change our minds. When Jesus tells us to stand firm on an issue, we have to stand firm. I have had to remind Matt many times: "We are trying to do what Jesus wants us to do. When we have to say 'no' to your requests, it's not because we <u>don't</u> love you. We say 'no' because we love you <u>so much</u>."

Just Testing

A few years ago, Matt was getting ready to leave home to serve some military time and we were reminiscing about the good old days. We had to laugh when he admitted there were times he asked us if he could do something with friends and was secretly hoping we'd say "no". He would then have an excuse for not going. Isn't that crazy? Why in the world did he even ask if he didn't want to go in the first place?

Looking back, I see, even though he sounded disappointed and angry when we said "no"; he was just testing us. What he found was he could always trust us to draw a line. He was acting as if he didn't want limits, yet he was trusting us to set the limits.

So Mom, don't let what your children say or threaten to do change what Jesus has asked you to do for them. It's our job to ask Jesus how to lead and guide them. Let them know Jesus will always be the reason decisions are made in your home. Expressions of love from your children or lack of them shouldn't make the decisions. If they do -- your children will soon learn that words of love can be withheld as a ransom. Early on in life, they will learn to use them as a tool to manipulate you into doing what they want you to do. Love them enough to say "no" and stick with it.

If They Loved Me...They'd Listen to Me

Oh, isn't that a good one? If they loved me, they'd listen to me. Don't we all yearn for that to be true! When I was pregnant with Matt, I knew that's what <u>my</u> child would want to do. He'd want to listen to my every word. He'd treasure my advice and consider everything out of my mouth as wisdom. I kept thinking of the woman in Proverbs 31. I loved the verse where it said, "...and her children will arise up and call her blessed..." In my head I could hear our

child say, "Oh Mom, you're so wise. Please tell me what to do. I know I can trust your advice."
It's true. It did happen. Matt did cling to my every word. That is, until the first time he was out on his daily crawling expedition and reached for something he wasn't supposed to touch. I said, "No". He looked back at the intriguing object and then back to me. He then reached for it anyway. That was my taste of the 'real world' of motherhood. No - our children don't always listen to us!

Years of Wisdom to Share

By the time Matt became a teen, I had stored up years of wisdom to share with him. I knew he'd want to listen so he, too, could become wise. It says so right in the Bible. Proverbs 13:10 says, "...wisdom is found in those who take advice." I was sure he would want to take my advice and benefit from all those years of my experience.
Alas, my plans were interrupted as puberty arrived at our home. During this time of enlightenment, Matt thought he knew everything there was to know about everything there was. My wisdom wasn't necessarily something he deeply desired or even sought. Once again, those feelings that maybe he really didn't love me began to surface. After all, if he loved me, he'd listen to me.
When Matt didn't listen to me, I was hurt. I got angry. I felt like pulling back and not even speaking to him, let alone sharing wisdom with someone who didn't want it. "Fine. Let him find out the hard way." became a tempting phrase of my heart. Yet I knew the Scriptures also instructed parents to train and instruct their children and bring them up in the loving discipline of the Lord (Ephesians 6:4).
How can I do it when he won't even listen? Tying him to the kitchen chair until he listened looked like an appealing solution. Then one day, I came upon a Scripture Paul wrote to the people of Corinth (2 Corinthians 1:12). In telling them how to deal with others he said this: "...Our conscience testifies that we have conducted ourselves in the world *(and our home)* and especially in our relations with you *(and our children)*, in the holiness and sincerity that are from God. We have not done so according to worldly wisdom but according to God's grace." *(Words in italics are mine.)*
I had to ask myself, "Does my conscience testify I am conducting myself in my home and with my child, in the

holiness and sincerity that comes from God?" This means I am always asking Jesus to keep my heart pure and in line with His desires. Am I trying to force my child to listen because I want to control or manipulate him? Or am I trying to share wisdom with him to draw him to Jesus?

If I can truly say I am sharing with the right motives (with holiness and sincerity), let's look at the last sentence of this Scripture to see what it says about how I am to share this wisdom. It says, "We have not done so according to worldly wisdom but according to God's grace." Is that how we are sharing our wisdom with our children? Not the way the world says but according to God's grace.

Well, how does the world share wisdom? To some parents the world says: "You're the boss! Just holler louder than they do!" To other parents it may say: "Who says you have any wisdom to share. Children are individuals with rights and shouldn't have any of your ideas forced on them. Let them decide what to do."

Now, we know neither of those are true. This is the world's way of dealing with our children. As Christians, we know God has commanded us to teach and instruct our children and to do it in a loving manner (Ephesians 6:4). So, how can we do this? James 3:17 (TLB) tells us, "But the wisdom that comes from heaven is first of all pure and full of quiet gentleness, then it is peace loving and courteous. It allows discussion and is willing to yield to others; it is full of mercy and good deeds. It is wholehearted and straight forward and sincere." This is how we can share our wisdom in God's grace. We can 'pray before we say' to ensure the wisdom we are sharing with our children is pure and full of quiet gentleness. When we pray first, then our wisdom will be courteous and willing to yield to others by allowing discussion. By God's grace, our words will be full of mercy, straight forward and sincere. Isn't God's way of sharing wisdom beautiful? Can't you see how it would bring peace as you deal with your children?

Am I _always_ able to share wisdom God's way in my own home, with my own child? No, I admit I'm not. Sometimes I just charge out there and blast him with words. "You need to do this!" "I can't believe you did that!" But, my _goal_ is to share any wisdom with Matt -- God's way. I am striving to ask Him first. I'm daily asking Jesus to help me stop and pray before I say, so the wisdom I have comes from heaven not from the world -- and not from me.

Now remember: Just because we do everything God asks us to do, our children still possess the free will to choose to listen to or reject our wisdom. All I know is that I want to do all I can to obey God and be the mother He wants me to be.

Yes, when Matt listens to me, it does make me feel good and maybe even loved. I also know even if he chooses not to listen to what I say, I'm not going to center my love for him or his love for me on that issue.

Can't Buy Me Love

Sometimes we try to buy the love of our children with things. We want them to have the right tennis shoes and name brand jeans like everyone else. Working Moms seem especially susceptible to this temptation. I remember I often had feelings of guilt from being away from Matt so much of the day, so buying things could easily have become a way to make up for the lack of time spent with him.

We may even try to buy their love by being permissive -- by cutting them slack in the behavior department. When we're working, it seems we're only with them for a few short hours each day, so we hate to spend the whole time hollering at them. We don't want to have them mad at us when we have so little time with them. When we try to buy love with permissiveness; discipline suffers. When discipline suffers; ultimately the child suffers and so does the entire family.

You Loved Me No Matter What

Yes, I'm the first to admit it. When Matt had an 'ideal' day, I was in heaven. It was a day when he didn't fuss at getting dressed or say 'yuk' when vegetables were served at dinner. Oh, those days gave me a warm, satisfied feeling of being loved. It made me want to sit down and spend every waking minute with that precious, little child.

Then there were those less than ideal days. We battled over what to wear. We bristled at each other over dirty clothes on his floor. It seemed everything he did or said shouted to me, "I don't love you!" What else could I do to make this child love me? I had done everything I knew how to do. What did I do wrong?

Then a couple of years ago I clearly saw the answer. We were attending Matt's graduation from Army boot camp. He had survived several months of a drill sergeant screaming sweet, little nothings into his ear. Through that experience had developed a more mature, realistic view of life and of his parents. I decided to take advantage of all of his new found maturity and said, "Matt, I know I've made lots of mistakes. If you could name one thing I did right as a Mom, what would it be?" He thought for a minute and said, "Mom, you loved me no matter what."

That was the most important thing to him -- that I loved him no matter what. In the final analysis, that is all he ever wanted -- to know I loved him no matter what. That was the answer to the question in my heart: "Does my child really love me?" His love for me wasn't necessarily based on what he said or did to prove his love but was based on a fact. The fact was he knew I'd love him no matter what he did or said.

He recognized there would be times when I would hate what he had done. There would be times when I was angry at what he said. He also knew I would always love him, no matter what happened. That was a fact and his love for me was based on that fact. My love for him was unconditional.

Isn't that exciting? I don't have to wait around for my child to prove he loves me. I just need to love my child as Jesus told me to love. The response to that love is up to my child.

How does Jesus tell us to love? I Corinthians 13:4-8a says, "Love is patient; love is kind. It does not envy, it does not boast, it is not proud. It is not rude, it is not self-seeking, it is not easily angered, it keeps no record of wrongs. Love does not delight in evil but rejoices with the truth. It always protects, always trusts, always hopes, always perseveres. Love never fails...." This is how we are to love our children -- no matter what. How they love us back is up to them.

No Substitute

Being loved is very important, isn't it? It makes us feel great. We think it even makes Jesus feel closer when someone close to us loves us. Someone once told me it puts arms to Jesus when a real person hugs us. There may be some truth to that statement, however, I want to tell you there is no substitute for Jesus' love in your life. Don't try to fill the Jesus-shaped vacuum with the love of your children, your husband or other people. Although their love is also important in our lives, don't let it try to substitute for the love Jesus has for you.

Human beings will eventually let you down. This is why they are called human -- so we remember they are not perfect. Someday your children might treat you as if they don't love you. If you are basing your entire 'love life' on humans, you will be hurt when they don't love you the way you need to be loved. Jesus has that daily, minute-by-minute, unfailing love for you no one else has.

If we go back to the Bible and look at Revelation chapter 2, we can obtain some insight into love. John was writing to the people of Ephesus sharing the words of encouragement and warning Jesus spoke. Verse 2-5 says, "I know how many good things you are doing. I have watched your hard work and your patience......You have patiently suffered for Me without quitting. Yet there is one thing wrong; you don't love Me as at first! Think about those times of your first love (how different now!) and turn back to Me again...(TLB)". Jesus was referring to their love for Him. The people of Ephesus were doing great things but forgot who they should love first -- Jesus.

Is that what has happened in your life, too? Have you lost your first love -- your love for Jesus. If this is true, today is the day to return to Jesus. Make Him the first love in your life. When He becomes first in your life, you will be able to love your children with His kind of love.

If Jesus is the first love in your life, you will always have the love of Jesus to carry you through, even when others don't say or show their love. His love should be the most important love in your life. There is no substitute for Jesus' love.

Love is Based on Jesus

If they loved me -- they'd act like it. They'd say it. They'd listen to me. No -- there's a chance they might not. Remember love is not based on reactions. Love is based on Jesus.

Love your children the way Jesus loves you. Keep pointing your children to Jesus so they have an example of the kind of love to have in their own lives. Then, Mom -- leave the rest to Jesus.

Let's join each other in prayer:

Father, You know how important being loved is to me. It seems to be the fuel that keeps me going when I feel like giving up. At times I have felt so lonely and unloved. Help me to see that I need to love You first. Help me to love you more than anyone in my life. Your love will fill me up to overflowing so I can love my family with Your love.

In your Son's name,
Amen

Spend some time alone with Jesus on these questions:

1. Do you ever feel rejected by your children? How does it make you feel?

2. Read Revelation 2:2-5. Write down what Jesus speaks to your heart.

   Who would you say is the 'first love' of your life? How could making Jesus your 'first love' change your life?

3. Do you think it's possible to love your children 'no matter what'? It's only possible through the power of Jesus Christ. Write a prayer asking Him to help you love your children unconditionally.

7

I Want to be the Best Mom in the World...

And I Am !!

This might sound a little conceited but it's true. I want to be the best Mom in the world -- and I am!
Now, I haven't always felt this way. . .

I Felt Inadequate

After Matt was born, I quickly saw my inadequacies. I was a nurse at the time, so you would think I had all the skills necessary to excel in the 'mommyhood' profession. I have to be truthful with you. I was scared to death of being a Mom. Oh, I knew how to hold him correctly and bathe him but what about all the rest I was supposed to know how to do? I was scared of failing at the one thing women were 'naturally' supposed to know how to do. I didn't just naturally know how to be a Mom. It was hard work for me.

I knew how to be a nurse. When I went to work -- doctors cooperated with me, patients listened to my wisdom and those I supervised, respected my position. I knew what to do at work. I was competent at my job. When I got home, it seemed as if no one listened to me, I definitely didn't have much wisdom and I felt totally incompetent. I didn't know how to be a Mom. All the training in the world doesn't prepare you for the task.

As I look back now, I believe that was one of the main reasons I worked after Matt was born. I took him to day care where people knew how to take care of children. I thought I couldn't do the job of raising Matt as well as they could. I didn't know all the right things to do. They did. They were the experts!

101

He Will Never Leave You nor Forsake You

Moms -- listen carefully. I have come to realize that thinking someone else could raise my child better than I could, was a misconception -- even a bold faced lie of Satan. You don't have to be an expert to be the best Mom in the world. You only have to be willing to let Jesus teach and train you. He doesn't take off points for mistakes. He doesn't give demerits for bad decisions. There will be times when you feel inadequate. We all will have those times. This is a perfect opportunity to turn to Jesus.

I was reading in the Old Testament about the job Moses had of leading his people out of Egypt. Now, there was a man who probably felt inadequate if I ever saw one. Leading that many people, through so many problems, for such a long time would make anyone feel inadequate. He didn't think he was trained enough. He didn't think he was the guy for the job and even tried to push it off on someone else (much like I did). He finally agreed to tackle the job. He found that in the midst of the challenges that job presented, he had scores of opportunities to turn to God when he felt inadequate.

When Moses knew his life was coming to a close, he called Joshua to his side. Joshua was the one chosen to take over his work to lead the people of Israel into the Promised Land. What an overwhelming job it must have felt like to Joshua. How could he fill the shoes of Moses? In Deuteronomy 31:8, Moses said to Joshua: "The Lord Himself goes before you and will be with you; He will never leave you nor forsake you. Do not be afraid; do not be discouraged." Moses knew what he was saying was true because he had experienced God's faithfulness. He knew through experience, God would never leave him or forsake him.

Later after Moses' death, God spoke those same words directly to Joshua. "No one will be able to stand up against you all the days of your life. As I was with Moses, so I will be with you; I will never leave you or forsake you" (Joshua 1:5). He was saying, "You've watched me be faithful to Moses. I will do the same for you. This same promise is also yours."

Now, leading the people into the Promised Land was a monumental job. No wonder God said He would never leave him or forsake him. Moses and Joshua could never have done it on their own. Do you think your job as a mother is

102

any less important? Any less monumental? Of course not! Bringing up children to know Jesus and to understand His love is one of the most important jobs in the whole world. So, I believe this promise was not only for Moses and Joshua but also for us. He says to us, "Don't be afraid or discouraged in your job as a Mother. I will go before you and I'll be with you. I will never leave you or forsake you."

I Only Deserved One Child

Having only one child was a choice my husband and I made a number of years ago. We rationalized our decision with all the 'right' logical reasons: money, time, bringing another child into a crazy world. I believe I agreed to that decision partly because I just didn't feel adequate as a Mom. I didn't know the right way to raise one child -- so how could I think of having another?

For a long time, I felt if God really thought I was such a good Mom, He could have stepped in and given us more children. It's a true fact -- God is sovereign and could have done just that. I had seen other couples get pregnant even after sterilization procedures. It never happened to us, so therefore -- God must think I'm a terrible Mom, too. He must not trust me as much as He trusts other Moms or He would have trusted me with more children. You know -- the merit system. You get more because you are more worthy.

However, my theory disintegrated as I remembered this fact: women who don't care for their children don't just stop having more children because they don't care. On the other hand, a barren woman with the deepest desire for children doesn't just automatically start to bear children because she wants one? It's not fair. Shouldn't the best have the most? Wouldn't this be a logical way to run things? Well, I have to tell you. God doesn't necessarily work on the principle of human logic but He is sovereign, which makes His logic perfect.

God is Sovereign

Do you know what sovereign means? According to Webster's Dictionary it means He is *above or supreme to all others, supreme in power, rank and authority* [4] . Although the actual word, sovereign, does not appear in the Bible, the attributes of God referring to His sovereignty are numerous:

He is omnipotent -- all powerful. He has the ability to do whatever He wills. He is not bound by the laws of nature as we see when he multiplied the loaves and fishes and when he walked on water. Matthew 19:26 says, nothing is impossible for God.

He is omniscient -- all knowing. He knows all things about the past, present and future. His understanding has no limit (Psalm 147:5).

He is omnipresent -- present everywhere. There is no where God has not been. There is no event God has not already witnessed. Psalm 139:7 reminds us, "I can never be lost to your Spirit! I can never get away from God....."

He's Got the Big Picture

All of this says to me that God possesses the 'Big Picture'. He has a view of life from the day it began until the day it will end. Our view is more like tunnel vision. We only see what is happening now or what might have happened in the past.

Ephesians 1:8 (TLB) reads, "...and He has showered down upon us the richness of His grace -- for how well He understands us and knows what is best for us at all times." Isn't it reassuring to realize He knows and understands everything? He knows what is best for us. He knew long before Matt was born he was the very best child for me. Although our choice not to have more children was one which had an effect on our lives, He knew this one child was what I needed.

Do I always understand the rationale of God's choices? No, but I don't have to understand them to trust them. I trust He knows what is best for me.

---

[4] Webster's New World Dictionary of the American Language, David G. Guralnik, Editor in Chief, Wm Collins and World Pub Co, Inc., Cleveland and New York, 1976, p 1363.

This Applies to Others, Too

This same principle of sovereignty applies not just to me, but to other Moms, too. God knows just what Mom has just what child. Yes, abuse, neglect or mistreatment of a child all make Him very saddened. None the less, He is still in charge and makes no mistakes.

I am saying this is to ask you to be an encouragement to other Moms. I don't know about you -- but there have been times in my life when I left someone's home only to remark later, "That kid would straighten out if only she'd..." "Why doesn't she just..." or "If I were the Mom I'd ..."

From a distance, we seem to have all the answers for everyone else, don't we? The very best thing you can do for another Mom is to remember they are the best Mom in the world for their children. Now they may not act as if they are -- but it is a fact. Now your job is to help them to become the very best. These Moms need your encouragement, too. They may even need your help. They definitely need your prayers but they don't need your criticism. (Are you listening, Moms and Moms-in-law? You can be the best encouragers of the young Mothers in your life.)

I'm the Best Mom in the Whole World

When I say, "I'm the best Mom in the whole world!" -- there is no pride. I'm not saying, "I'm better than any other Mom or better because I do more for my child. What I am saying is: "I'm the best Mom in the whole world for Matt." It's true because God chose me to be Matt's Mom. No one else can do it like I can! There are many teachers. There are many surgeons. There is only one Mom for Matt.

(If your child is adopted, please remember God chose the mother who would physically bring your child into this world. He also chose you to be the best Mom in the world to raise your child to know Jesus and love Him. You are both very vital in the life of this child.)

Still Can't Get Those Words Out of Your Mouth?

Are you still having a difficult time believing it's true? Do you have a hard time saying, "I'm the best Mom in the world for my children." Don't be so tough on yourself. You're the best Mom in the world because God chose you -- not because of your abilities or talents. It's true because God chose you.

We all make mistakes. We all have regrets but I'll never regret that God chose me to be Matt's Mom. This makes me the very best Mom in the world. . . for Matt! This is the reason you are the very best Mom in the world. . . for your children!

The words in Jeremiah 1:5 (TLB) are music in my ears. "I knew you before you were formed within your mother's womb..." God knew your children before they were born. He also knew you before they were formed in your womb.

God doesn't make mistakes. He placed each child in your womb. He knew who you were, with all your weaknesses and strengths. He chose you because He knew you'd be the very best Mom in the whole world for that child.

Won't you join me in this prayer:

Dear Father, I want to thank You for choosing me to be the mother for_____. I know I've made mistakes. Please forgive me when I fall short. Help me to believe I'm the best Mom in the world for my children. I know You don't make mistakes and it was no mistake that You chose me to be their Mom. I trust You to teach me to be the kind of mother You want me to be.

In Jesus' name,
Amen

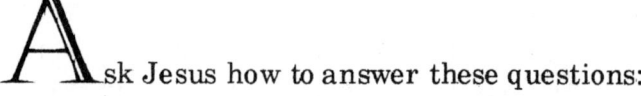sk Jesus how to answer these questions:

1. Moses was called to complete a monumental task. He must have felt overwhelmed at times. Has there been a time when you felt overwhelmed in your job of mothering? When?

2. Ephesians 1:8 (TLB) says, '...He has showered down upon us the richness of His grace - for how well He understands us and knows what is best for us at all times." Write in your own words what this verse means to you.

The Best Thing You Can Do for Your Children

Now that you <u>know</u> you're the best Mom in the world for your children, what is the best thing you can do for them? No -- it won't cost you money. No -- you can't get it in a store. The best thing you can do for your children is to have a personal relationship with Jesus Christ. You may have been sitting in a church pew most of your life or you may never have stepped inside a church. Either way -- you need Jesus. It's much more than just being in a church. It's a day to day walk with Him. As you get to know Jesus better and better, you will see Him provide all you need to be a great mother.

Why Do You Need This?

Romans 3:23 says, "...all have sinned and fall short of the glory of God." 'All' means you and me. Everyone of us fall short. This is why we all need Jesus.

Don't I Have to Get My Life Straight First?

Romans 5:8 tells us, "But God demonstrates His own love for us in this: While we were still sinners, Christ died for us." He didn't wait until we were good enough or got our lives straightened out before He got on the cross to die for us. He died for us while we were still sinners.

That is how He will take you today -- right now, just where you are in your life. You don't have to get good enough to come to know Jesus. You just need to realize that you need Him.

Is He Calling You?

The Bible tells us Jesus does the calling. By His Holy Spirit, He reaches out and touches our hearts. Revelation 3:20 says, "Here I am! I stand at the door and knock. If anyone hears My voice and opens the door, I will come in and eat with him, and he with Me." When we hear the call, we can respond to the work Jesus has already done in our hearts.

He Does the Changing

When you answer His call, He begins to change your life from the inside out. His power enables you to break old habits and change old ways. He is the changer of lives. He is the one who will enable you to be the kind of Mother your children need.

Give Your Children the Best Gift

The best gift you can give your children is the gift of your salvation. If Jesus has been speaking to your heart as you have read this book, won't you answer the call today. It will change your life.

You can do it right now, wherever you might be.
Open your heart to Jesus.

You can pray this simple prayer:

Dear Father,
I have felt You calling me and today I want to answer. I confess that I am a sinner and can do nothing to save myself. I believe You died for my sins and paid the price to set me free. Please forgive me. Help me to turn away from my old ways and live a new life for You. Thank You for promising me eternal life with You in heaven. Thank You for giving me the best gift to share with my children.
In Jesus' name
Amen

Where Are We Now?

It's been a few years since this book was published and we have had some changes in our lives, including more gray hair and a few additional years on the birthday calendar. Our son, Matt, turned 40 this year! (How did that happen?) Mike and I celebrated our 43rd anniversary! (How did we get that old?) After 14 years of marriage, we suffered through a painful divorce with our son. Through that time, I believe I experienced God lovingly pry my fingers off the hurtful situation and He is daily teaching me how to allow Him to heal the hearts of our family.

We are so proud of our son, Matt. He has grown into a wonderful man with a tender (yet strong and independent) side we have come to appreciate and admire more than ever before. For many years, I equated my success or failure as a Mom to how he 'turned out'. Don't we just love to do that? We puff up and feel a little proud at what a good job we have done when they get straight A's, marry the perfect wife or land an important job. We put on the 'I Must Be a Failure' t-shirt when they misbehave in public, make wrong choices or don't match up to our friends' children.

Believe me, being the best Mom in the world has nothing to do with the 'end product'...your child! It has to do with what God did. He chose you to be the Mom and that's what makes you the best Mom in the world for your child! That fact doesn't cease to exist because we stop feeling like the best...or maybe even think we're the worst!

Another thing that has not changed is the fact I am still a Mom (and always will be). I still make mistakes. I even find myself occasionally getting back on Regret Circle where I make a visit to the 'Coulda-Woulda-Shouldas'. That's when God reminds me I can't undo anything in the past but I can allow Him to do the forgiving, rebuilding and renewing in my heart... starting with today!

As Moms, we tend to spend so much time doing things for our children. We make sure they have lessons, sports and the right schools. We want them to learn the most and be the best. We buy them high tech toys, stylish clothes and new cars. We are doing all we can to help them succeed. We are doing whatever it takes to give them advantages we might not have had.

One thing I would say to you: It's not what you are doing for your children that matters... it's what you're being! You are being their Mom! No, you won't ever do it perfectly. You don't have to be perfect because everything you're not.....Jesus is!

So, don't be so hard on yourself. Just relax and be the best Mom in the world...for your child!

Consider yourself hugged!

Connie

Please write me and tell me how Jesus is blessing you as an imperfect vessel for His love to be delivered to your children.

Connie Gilbride   great.plains.ministry@sio.midco.net
Great Plains Ministry
5907 W Wren Pl
Sioux Falls, SD 57107

About the Author

Connie Gilbride was born and raised in the central plains of America. She trained as a registered nurse and worked in various medical fields during her 12 year career. During her 27 years of marriage to her husband Mike, she set up housekeeping in 15 states and two foreign countries. She spent 15 years as a military wife and seven years as a missionary.

Both Connie and Mike received intensive missionary and discipleship training through Son Shine Ministries International, an interdenominational missionary organization based in Texas. They spent two years as missionaries in Germany, with emphasis being ministry to the American military family. They also worked at the World Headquarters, in staff and missionary school positions and were integral members of retreat and teaching teams.

At Jesus' direction in 1992, they formed Great Plains Ministry. This resource ministry was formed to meet the needs of couples, families and individuals. Over the past 12 years of ministry, Connie has presented programs and retreats for women around America and overseas. Together, she and Mike have also ministered through marriage retreats and parenting classes.

Their son, Matthew, is 23 years old. He is currently employed as a computer software and hardware specialist with a firm in Buffalo, New York.

Connie is committed and dedicated to encouraging women in their God-given roles in the family and in pointing women to Jesus as their hope.